Insight Trading

Collaborating to transform the infrastructure that shapes society

by Nick Fleming and Susanne Cooper

Around the world, greater demands are being placed on cities, infrastructure and the resources that underpin economic development and prosperity.

Developers, owners and operators of public and private infrastructure face a greater challenge and responsibility to deliver assets, resources and services that fulfil these changing needs and community expectations. Leaders are faced with making big business and technology bets at a time when they are also striving to achieve more with less.

Without question, new solutions are called for.

This book answers the call. It shares insights and real case studies from project teams and organisations that are pioneering more sustainable, enduring and profitable solutions. How to shift thinking and business practices is the focus. Better placed effort (not more effort) is often what is required to achieve breakthrough solutions. Exciting new possibilities are within reach.

The authors

Nick Fleming has been a leading contributor to sustainable development for over 20 years, utilising his background in engineering, a PhD in sustainable water infrastructure, and qualifications and experience in strategic business leadership.
He brings diverse industry experience, working internationally across sectors including water, transport, mining, defence and natural resources. Nick has an aptitude for finding elegant solutions to complex problems, often working at the Board and executive level to develop pragmatic strategies and designs to sustain businesses, projects and communities. He is widely published and a recognised speaker. Nick was the Chief Sustainability Officer of Sinclair Knight Merz before becoming the Director of Business Innovation at Jacobs, also sitting on several industry bodies fostering sustainable infrastructure.

Susanne Cooper has 25 years of experience leading and working with multi-disciplinary teams and senior levels of organisations to achieve practical but innovative change for better outcomes, backed by technical rigour and incisive thinking. She is a recognised facilitator of innovative approaches to complex problems. Susanne combines her technical expertise in environmental science with the insights gained from strategy and policy development and project design at all levels of government and with private corporations across most industry sectors including water, natural resources, mining, energy, transport and chemicals. Susanne is currently a Principal sustainability and innovation strategist for Jacobs.

Insight Trading
Collaborating to transform the infrastructure that shapes society,
by Nick Fleming and Susanne Cooper.

ISBN 978-0-646-90325-5

Publisher
Jacobs Group (Australia) Pty Limited
100 Christie Street, St Leonards,
Sydney, New South Wales 2065 Australia
T +61 2 9928 2100

Acknowledgements

Insight Trading is the product of many years of experience working across the world with people who are determined to achieve great things, for themselves and the organisations they represent as well as for the wider community. While this presents far too many people to name here, we would like to acknowledge and thank those people with the drive, courage and tenacity to seek out better solutions, providing the stories and insights upon which this book is based.

We are particularly grateful to the people who gave freely of their time and wealth of knowledge to provide feedback to refine and enhance this book. They included John Elkington (Volans), Pedro Rodrigues De Almeida (World Economic Forum), David Loggia (Carmingnac Gestion), Stephen Selwood (NZ Council for Infrastructure Development), Professor John Thwaites (Monash Sustainability Institute and ClimateWorks Australia) and Ben Waters (GE Ecomagination), and those from across the global operations of Sinclair Knight Merz (SKM): Peter Corrie, Keith Marr, Sheldon Krahe, Alastair Moffat, Gillian Sisk, Ben Stapleton, Lisa Woolhouse, Simon Yacoub and Peter Young.

We must also acknowledge the support and encouragement of the communications and production team. Tim Dilnot, Jessica Harrison, Natalia Thompson (Agile & Associates) and Carol Mackay (Mackay Branson design) translated our ideas, bringing the words to life on the page.

Finally, thanks to Santo Rizzuto and Paul Dougas, as former CEOs of SKM, who together with Chairman Peter Scott and the business unit management teams maintained their ongoing commitment to the firm's values, strategies and corporate purpose – to make a positive and enduring impact on the world. This has made this work possible and its future application exciting for all concerned.

Contents

One

We can do so much better

This book is about transformation – in mindsets, action and outcomes.

Why transformation? Because it's clear we're living through a major shift in human thought and action. How we think about, plan and construct our future is changing.

In historical terms, this shift is dramatic and fast-moving. In just the last decade, global leaders have started acting on the need to reorganise our economies. At the same time, consumers and communities have become more aware, connected and active in exercising their power to change the world around them. Yet the prevailing forms of development are still falling short; they simply aren't achieving the steep changes in productivity and social outcomes that are required.

So as we see it, the problem is two-fold: current forms of development remain largely unsustainable, and we're missing readily available opportunities to achieve a much greater return for business and society on the investment of our collective time, intellect and resources.

The solutions exist

Finding ways to address this problem and the challenges of the evolving operating environment can certainly be daunting. But it's not impossible – indeed, far from it.

Smarter, simpler, cheaper, more effective solutions are available right now, even for our most complicated business and development challenges.

This includes solutions in government that ensure investment occurs in the right projects, making each public dollar go further to reduce costs while increasing value, even with conventional technologies. It means solutions for business that generate shareholder value in a way that also creates long-term benefit for communities and societies.

We call them sustainable solutions.

Sharing our insights to magnify their impact

We wrote this book because we know the solutions exist, and are being employed by pioneering organisations around the world. But they are not complex or expensive technologies; they are motivating, achievable and replicable ways of thinking and problem solving. Yet these approaches are seemingly hidden from view, so we want to bring them into the light for all to see.

In particular, this book is for the planners, investors, engineers, owners and operators of the private and public infrastructure that has such a profound and enduring influence on the form and function of society.

By sharing our insights and experiences, we hope to inform, motivate and equip people to conceive and deliver more sustainable infrastructure.

What lies within these pages?

Using real-world examples, we explain a different approach to conceiving and implementing higher-value solutions, so that organisations can apply more genuine and effective responses to the sustainability challenge. It involves looking at the bigger picture, consciously collaborating for real results, and delivering a realistic project vision and a strategy that sticks.

We show that it takes redirection of effort rather than the application of additional effort to achieve more sustainable outcomes, and that most organisations already possess the ability to succeed in this.

Finally, we offer our advice and experience on finding and applying the right mix of expertise, selecting the right sustainability tools and reporting on your actions and achievements for maximum impact.

We hope you finish this book feeling optimistic about our collective ability to transform how we construct and operate the assets and systems that matter to us most. More than that, we want to spur you on to new thought and action across your sphere of influence – because we can all do so much better.

Making sense of
Sustainability...

Over the past few
decades the term
"sustainability" has
been so scrutinised,
interpreted, hijacked
and distorted that,
in many cases, it has
become a source of
frustration and a
barrier to dialogue –
and thus to progress.

So, right from the outset, it's important we explain how we think about sustainability, and what meaning this book holds.

Firstly, many inter-connected *sustainability issues* threaten societal stability and prosperity. They include financial turmoil, high levels of public debt, economic restructuring, rising economic disparity, growing water scarcity, energy security, food security, a changing climate, ocean degradation, and political polarisation. Of course, the list goes on, but you get the point.

Finding and designing effective ways of dealing with these issues in order to survive and thrive is the *sustainability challenge* that we jointly face. It's also a major source of business opportunity.

So our view is that *sustainable development* involves cultivating the organisations, infrastructure, goods and services to meet the sustainability challenge – simultaneously creating value for business and society, now and over the longer term.

Creating this value requires solutions that are "fit for purpose" now and also "fit for the future". To be "fit", we believe *sustainable solutions* must be conceived to:

- maintain the natural systems on which we all depend,

- reduce risks and constraints on development,

- reduce capital and operating costs,

- maintain an organisation's legal and social licence to operate, and

- deliver substantially better and longer-lasting social and environmental outcomes.

Two

Success is taking a different shape

New issues and drivers in the market need an integrated response.

It's not just efficient solutions we need – it's *effective* solutions.

It means focusing on "doing the right things" not just "doing things right".

"The infrastructure 'problem'
can't be ignored just because
it's complicated...we have to deal
with the complexities of reality."

Sir Rod Eddington, former British Airways CEO
and current chair of Infrastructure Australia[1]

1   SKM *achieve*, 2009

Increasing complexity

The context in which we design, establish and operate projects and businesses is changing. A suite of emerging issues and new drivers of success across industry sectors and all geographies is impacting the way we scope, design, deliver and operate projects and businesses. It affects us all, as no project, organisation or industry sector will be untouched by the shifts that are underway. In many cases, these changes will be transformative.

The issues and drivers include the declining condition of the natural environment, resource depletion, and the need to reduce greenhouse gas emissions and adapt to a changing climate. Drivers also relate to social equity, security of food, energy and water supplies, coupled with changing patterns of mobility and migration. It provides a very different context in which to deliver and operate infrastructure which must not only be fit for purpose now, but also fit for the future. We're challenged to re-think the purpose and function of the infrastructure we build now because it must sustain our activities and needs for the next several decades.

The pace and scale of change we're experiencing is evident in the language and terminology now used across government, business and communities. We speak of "virtual water", "total carbon footprint" and "social licence to operate" – terms that were largely unheard of a decade ago. This represents a more complex reality for projects and organisations than ever before.

There is another challenging facet to this situation. The issues and drivers rarely occur in isolation from each other; indeed, there are often closely interrelated. The organisations and project teams that recognise this are overcoming piecemeal approaches to conceive integrated, sustainable and successful solutions.

Time, cost and quality have been and still are critical project drivers, but new drivers continue to emerge, creating a more complex operating environment for projects and organisations. The trend will continue, but who knows what additional factors will be present in 2020? As they emerge and become defined, more active management will be needed. A fragmented or ad hoc response equates to mismanagement and risk – which will inevitably impact on time, cost and quality.

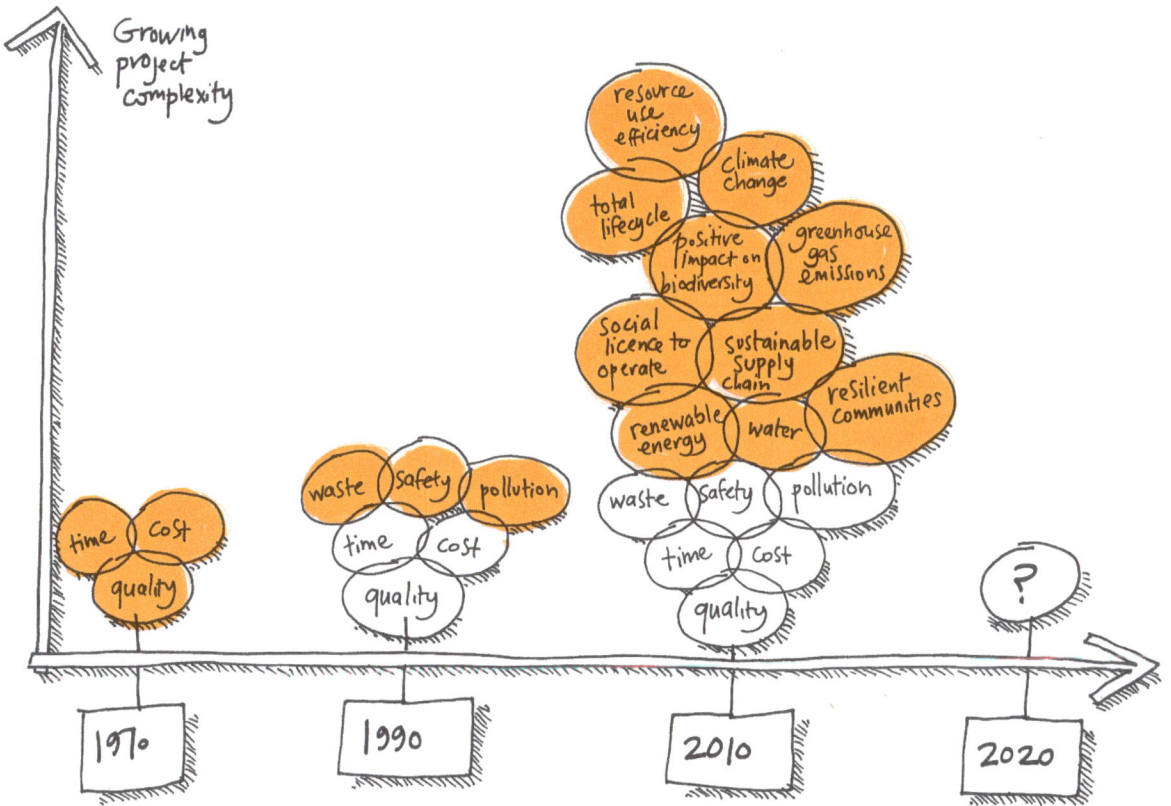

Growing project complexity

1970: time, cost, quality

1990: waste, safety, pollution, time, cost, quality

2010: resource use efficiency, climate change, total lifecycle, positive impact on biodiversity, greenhouse gas emissions, social licence to operate, sustainable supply chain, resilient communities, renewable energy, water, waste, safety, pollution, time, cost, quality

2020: ?

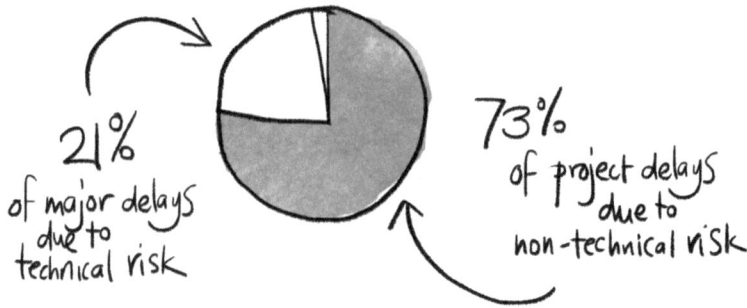

21% of major delays due to technical risk

73% of project delays due to non-technical risk

Changing expectations

The expectations of local communities and other stakeholders are also changing; the operational activities and behaviours that were once acceptable are no longer. We're witnessing the systematic translation of these heightened social expectations into legislation, regulatory requirements and industry standards. At the same time, political decisions about sensitive issues and projects are subject to greater scrutiny, with investors and insurers increasingly alert to the risks they pose. What was once an optional "feel good" activity or the right thing to do is increasingly driven by formal legal requirements to become a "need to do".

Failing to address these issues creates real strategic and operational business risks for a project or entire organisation. Pursuing sustainable project and business outcomes is therefore consistent with business excellence, long-term business resilience and preservation of shareholder value.

This is clearly evident from recent research which found 73 per cent of the world's 190 largest oil and gas projects experienced major project delays because of "above-ground" or non-technical risk. Just 21 per cent of major delays were caused by technical risk.[2] Issues such as stakeholder resistance and environmental concerns were the big barriers to progress for these projects.

2   D. Snashall, (2010) *Keeping oil and gas mega projects moving – grappling with non-technical risk.* Environmental Risk Management – ERM.www.erm.com/Analysis-and-Insight/Articles/Keeping-oil-and-gasmega-projects-moving--grappling-with-Non-Technical-Risk/

Maintaining a social licence to operate

Profitability and a legal licence to operate are no longer sufficient measures of a company's viability and success.

Social needs define markets – and social issues and community values define the laws. Today, the public has a heightened awareness of social issues and is actively shaping the political response. This influences organisations' needs to gain and maintain their legal licence to operate. But organisations also require a "social licence to operate" – meeting the expectations of society that are real and present but which are yet to be translated into regulations or market signals.

Meeting these expectations about organisational behaviour will gain community and stakeholder acceptance and trust. Of course, the conditions attached to a social licence will vary across communities, regions, project phases and life cycles. Furthermore, a social licence is easily lost and hard to regain, particularly in a connected world where people can quickly unite around issues of concern.

Maintaining trust and social licence is a whole-of-organisation and whole-of-project-life responsibility. Importantly, a social licence is an outcome based on a thorough understanding of the interests and issues of communities and other stakeholders on local, national and even international scales. It is earned over time and informally bestowed by stakeholders that include local communities and political organisations as well as international non-government groups.

New communication and networking technologies add a volatile dimension to gaining and maintaining a social licence. Better informed, organised and networked community groups with a grievance can now access social media channels to communicate their concerns and mobilise action. Local issues can quickly escalate to national or international prominence. Withdrawal of your social licence quickly follows. Indeed, the notion of "community" has itself become broader, often involving a loosely connected and informed network of individuals and organisations (or stakeholders) that can span entire continents and cultures.

Take the example The risks of failing to understand the need for a social licence is provided by an Australian company, Gunns Limited. It was Australia's largest integrated forestry products company just a few years ago, but today it no longer exists. What happened to change its fortunes so quickly? It's worth spending the time to explain.

A critical downward turning point occurred in 2005, when Gunns announced the site of a proposed US$2.6 billion pulp mill. Like most forestry companies, Gunns had dealt with community opposition to its activities for decades, so it wasn't greatly concerned with initial opposition to the pulp mill. But things had changed – the announcement triggered concern by community and environmental groups about issues such as the suitability of the site, the old growth forest feedstock the mill would process and the use of poisonous bait (which takes a big toll on native wildlife) to protect replacement tree seedlings.

Local lobby groups coordinated their efforts with international forest action groups. They initially targeted the Japanese paper mills which were major customers of Gunns, followed by the company's European business partners. Their campaigning shifted to investors, with shareholder resolutions submitted to the banks to shift their investment preferences away from Gunns. Rather than engaging with their opponents, Gunns was hostile, making it an even bigger community target. Despite this, it ultimately gained a legal licence to construct the pulp mill. However, this didn't make the process any easier. The company encountered ongoing financing difficulties as the banks withdrew their support and project timeline delays were incurred. Changes had to be made.

In 2009, a new CEO was appointed to try to turn fortunes around. By 2010, Gunns announced it would use 100 per cent plantation timber for the pulp mill and would cease using bait to protect seedlings. But the rot had set in. Losing accreditation by the Forestry Stewardship Council for its woodchip products meant it lost its major export market in Japan, as Japanese paper makers decided to accept only FSC-accredited products.

In May 2010, under massive pressure from major institutional investors and with the share price at 26 cents (5 per cent of its 2005 value), the Executive Chairman announced his retirement. It was clear the legal environmental approvals he'd fought for and won were irrelevant without a social licence to operate.

These events illustrate how Gunns fundamentally mismanaged its community, customer and investor relations. By March 2012, the share value of Gunns had plummeted to just 16 cents. Shareholders launched a class action against the company for its failure to disclose material information about its significant deterioration in its likely financial performance. In September 2012, Gunns was placed into administration after its bankers withdrew their support for efforts to raise new capital.

Gunns is more than a case study of how not to deal with community protest. It goes to the heart of an outmoded business model, weak corporate governance, poor recognition of supply chain risks, and the potential for local community protest to be escalated into the international arena. All were key ingredients in Gunns losing its social licence.

Many organisations fail to recognise the existence or importance of their social licence until communities take it away. Corporate responsibility programs have emerged in reaction to external pressure to improve the reputations of firms, but these are treated largely as an expense. They risk being perceived as just a cost of doing business, as impact mitigation can be seen as a necessary cost to make projects "less bad".

The more progressive business and project managers are recognising this and responding. *"The technical issues we can solve. We've been designing roads, pipelines and power networks for decades. Sure, there may be engineering challenges, but it's not often we can't sort them out. It's the social and environmental issues that are much harder and need more attention"* is an increasingly common sentiment.

Level of social licence

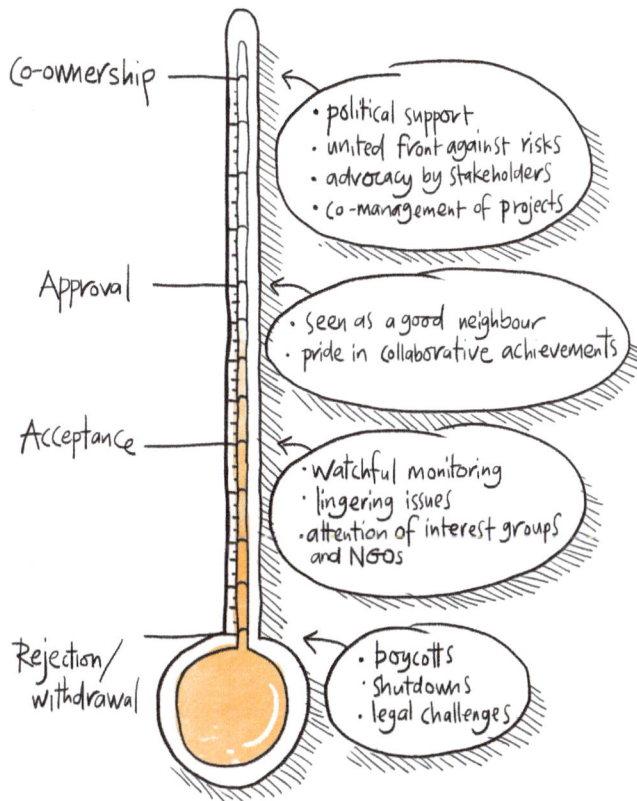

Co-ownership
- political support
- united front against risks
- advocacy by stakeholders
- co-management of projects

Approval
- seen as a good neighbour
- pride in collaborative achievements

Acceptance
- watchful monitoring
- lingering issues
- attention of interest groups and NGOs

Rejection/withdrawal
- boycotts
- shutdowns
- legal challenges

Adapted from R.G. Boutilier, and I. Thomson,(2011). *Modelling and Measuring the Social Licence to Operate: Fruits of a Dialogue between Theory and Practice.*

Managing for more than efficiency

While efficiency-driven initiatives are worthwhile, other issues and drivers of change demand a more fundamental review of projects and business models.

Take the example

"We dodged a bullet; it was that close." These were the words of the manager of a water utility that nearly ran out of water to supply a city of over 2 million people. Perhaps surprisingly, flooding had triggered the near disaster. *"We thought we had a very efficient and reliable potable water system, that is, until the flood closed the industrial and warehouse areas round the port."* This meant supplies of chemicals required for water treatment couldn't be accessed. *"Adding to the woes – many treatment plants were isolated by the floodwaters, so staff and supplies had to be helicoptered in."* This would not normally have been a problem, yet in the midst of the flood crisis, every available helicopter was in action, with the priority given to search and rescue activities. *"We had to argue our case against other priorities, and all the essential services were in the same boat."* But the problems didn't stop there. The whole system underpinning essential services was unravelling. A search for another chemical required for treatment revealed that the production facilities of the main supplier of this chemical were flooded. The third (and final) supplier had run out of stock the previous day; being the only operating chemical supplier, they had been overwhelmed by the increased demand. Other essential services were also affected. Loss of power and failures in the back-up battery systems had undermined the mobile phone system at the time when it was needed most.

The reflections from this event are noteworthy. The utility manager observed: *"We never planned for such a catastrophic scenario. No one predicted that the problems would compound, nor so quickly. It made us realise we manage to averages and for efficiency. We simply couldn't cope with a sudden shock to the system. We're now in the process of re-thinking what risk and resilience means, right through-out the system and supply chain."*

This potentially catastrophic event highlights the gap between an efficient system designed to perform well under past and predictable operating conditions, and one that is also effective. There's no doubt that improving efficiency delivers cost and resource-reduction benefits under normal operating conditions, and in one sense is more sustainable. But at local and global scales, delivering more of the same but at a faster rate or in greater volumes with less raw material inputs simply won't be enough to meet community, regulatory and political requirements, nor to manage risks outside of normal or average operating conditions.

Solutions must now be *effective*, not just efficient. It's clear we need to be doing more than "doing things right" (that is, improving efficiency). We must be *doing the right things* to achieve the economic decoupling and transformation needed to deliver infrastructure systems and solutions that are fundamentally more effective now, and in the future, when the challenges will inevitably be greater.

That doesn't necessarily mean *more* effort, but it does mean redirected effort.

By this we mean organisations and project teams should proactively identify and address the most relevant issues and drivers of success from the outset, rather than reacting to risks and protests when they emerge. Business strategies and project solutions that provide sustainable financial, social and environmental outcomes provide a platform for long-term credibility and enhanced business performance. Indeed, whether and how these factors are addressed will determine the value ascribed to assets, projects and organisations.

Effective, not just efficient, solutions will increasingly be needed. Improving the efficiency of existing systems does not guarantee that they are also the "right" systems – that is, systems or solutions that are suited to emerging conditions and future requirements. Indeed, it may be causing the systems to become more rigid and prone to collapse when operating conditions change. So a thoughtful and robust process is required to properly scope "the right thing"(effectiveness) – before focusing on "delivering it right" (efficiency).

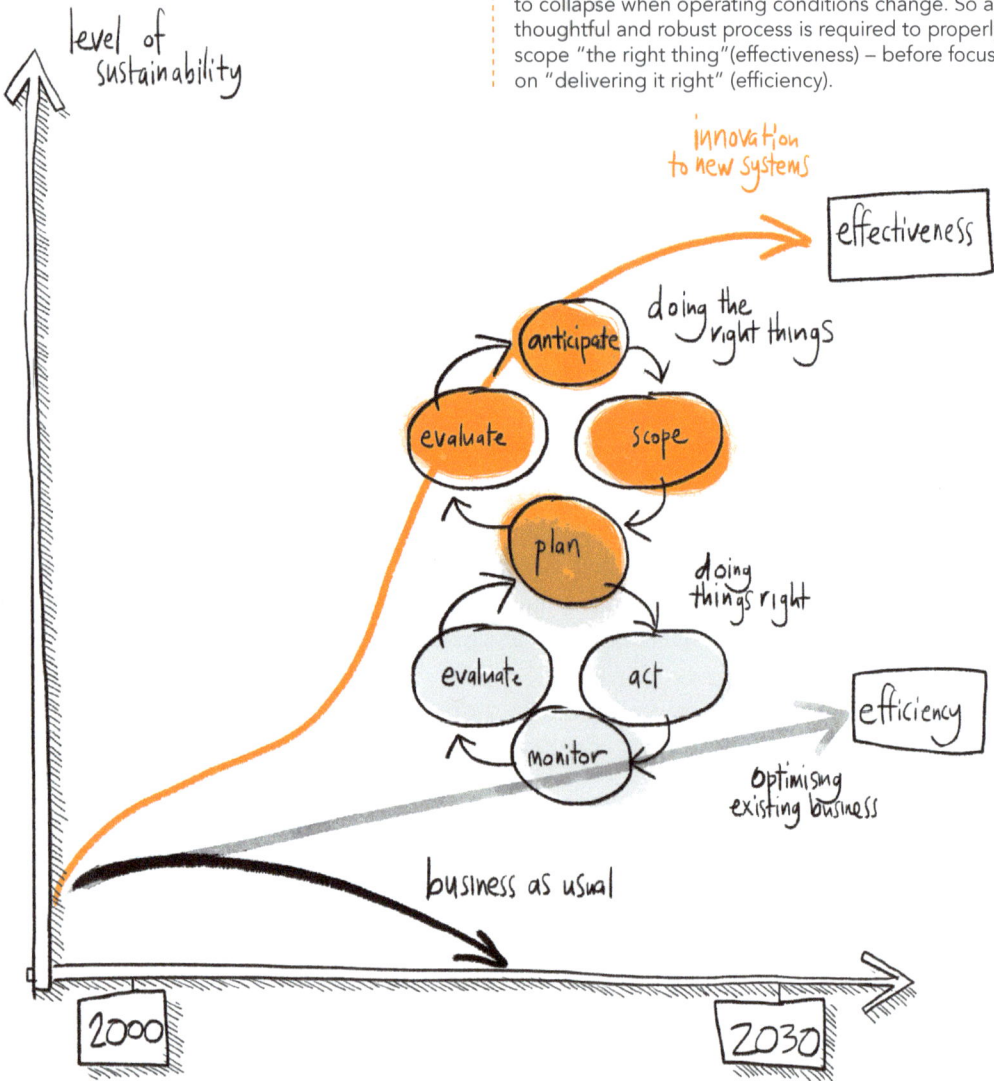

level of sustainability

innovation to new systems

effectiveness

anticipate

doing the right things

evaluate

scope

plan

doing things right

evaluate

act

efficiency

monitor

optimising existing business

business as usual

2000

2030

USEFUL QUESTIONS

- What has been a significant change in the context for your projects or organisation over the past few years? Have any of the flow-on effects been unexpected or unanticipated?

- How would you assess your current social licence to operate?

- How might conditions for your project or business change in the foreseeable future, and what potential consequences of these changes should you be planning for?

- How is a project you are currently working on both efficient and effective?

- How resilient and adaptable is the essential infrastructure of your supply chain, industry or city?

Three

Redefining value

The attributes of "value" have changed.

Success demands more than saving on design and construction costs.

Intangibles can make or break your project.

"Resources are not.
They become."

Erich Zimmermann,
World Resources and Industries, 1933

Who determines value?

The notion of "value" is not inherent, absolute or fixed for resources, the environment, infrastructure or our activities. Value is *assigned*. So who assigns value? We all do – as individuals, as members of a community or an organisation. What we value also changes over time, and it changes depending on our perspective and role. An asset owner will usually determine value differently from a community member, although we see these different perspectives of value increasingly finding common ground and areas of mutual interest.

Value can be expressed as the relationship between cost and performance. The higher the performance of a business or asset for the same level of investment or cost, the higher its value will be.

A key goal for us in writing this book was to highlight that what constitutes "acceptable performance" of organisations and projects is changing. This is the logical consequence of evolving social expectations and regulatory responses, which have triggered different perceptions of risk and value.

So the notion that value is being redefined should not be unexpected or surprising. What *is* surprising is that so many business decisions are still driven by financial models structured around narrowly-scoped criteria that generate a limited perspective of value governed by short-term shareholder returns and reducing capital cost – at a time when investors and stakeholders are expecting so much more.

What do you value?

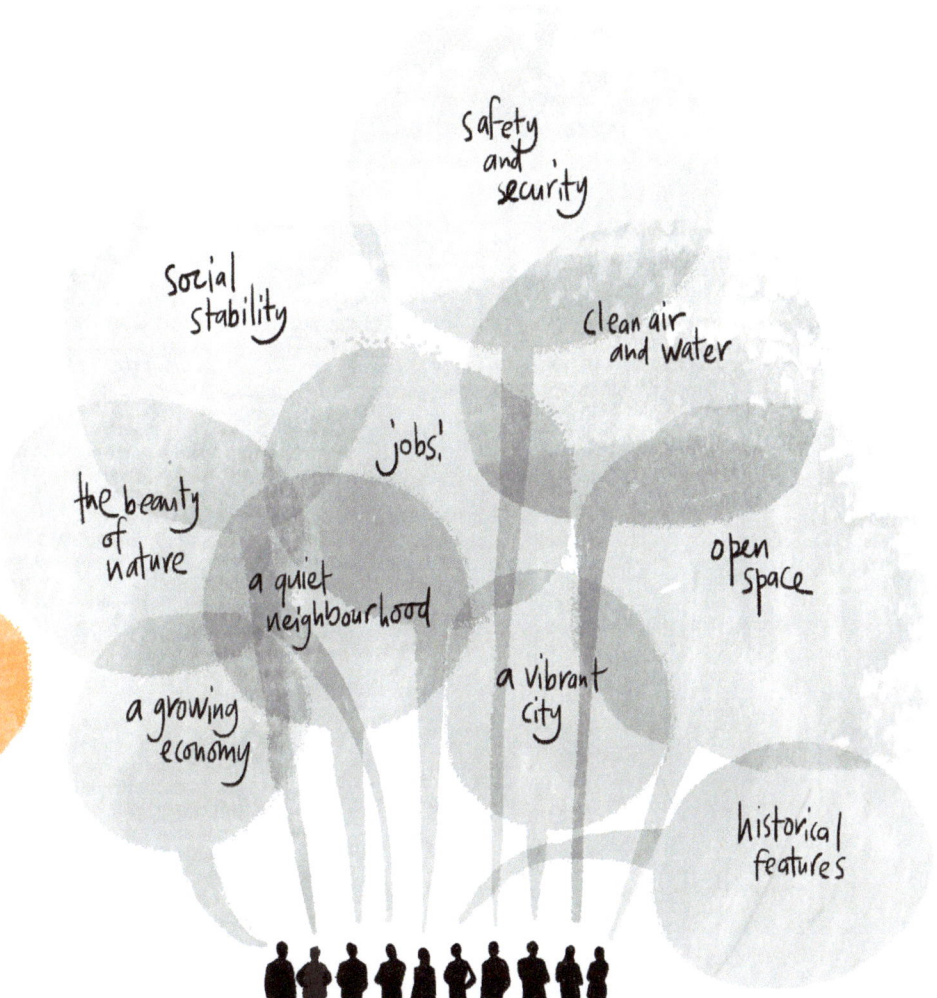

safety
and
security

social
stability

clean air
and water

jobs!

the beauty
of
nature

a quiet
neighbourhood

open
space

a growing
economy

a vibrant
city

historical
features

Take the example

"That was a great outcome – and one I wasn't expecting" was the surprised comment from the manager of a major works program charged with upgrading wastewater infrastructure across a capital city. His comment came at the end of a session to review options to upgrade a key water treatment plant. The plant's pumps were ageing and inadequate for the growing population, posing real risks of spills and overflows in a community already mistrustful after a history of odours and breakdowns. When we arrived on the project, the project team was veering toward constructing additional pumps at the plant, setting aside large areas of the site as compensation basins to capture any spills or overflow. The design task was almost decided…but not quite.

The senior engineers were not happy and voiced their interest in exploring other options. *"We can build more of the same, but somehow this just doesn't feel like the right decision. We need to re-think this."* Leading a review of the initial design, we revealed some very real risks and costs with the original solution. While exansion of the plant was likely in the next decade it already occupied a large portion of its urban site with little extra space available. The operating costs of additional pumps were also considerably higher, including increased energy use, greenhouse emissions and maintenance.

Working with the project team, we developed a very different and ultimately better solution. A simpler design with a smaller footprint that provided greater reliability and reduced maintenance costs would deliver a net positive return to the plant's owners over its lifetime, although the initial capital outlay was higher. It also freed up a third of the site for future expansion and reduced the probability of spills, which would improve the historically low levels of credibility, trust and support within the community.

The team was keen to communicate the alternative to the senior managers in a way that demonstrated a clear business case compared with other options. Pivotal to their success was assessing performance against all the material issues that were broader than a model narrowly defined according to capital and operating costs ("capex" and "opex"). This shifted the focus of the discussion among senior managers. One manager summed it up: *"We all know this option comes at a higher capital cost. But it represents what we should be aiming for. We don't have the budget right now, so I suggest some minor works over the next year as a temporary measure, and then implementation in full."*

What was the turning point for this team? It was exposing the total picture of value, and all the factors contributing to it. The managers could see how cost reduction and value uplift could be achieved. *"We didn't think including the broader factors and intangibles in the assessment would really make that much difference. But it showed our thinking was wide of the mark. I think it was because we had never tried to systematically assess and value these issues before. It demonstrated that we need to be thinking of not just meeting current demand but also about how these plants will need to function in future."*

The changing value boundary

In our work we're seeing project boundaries shifting ever outwards. Issues, assets and impacts once considered "intangible" and external to the project are now internalised as a core part of project delivery, and within its sphere of influence and responsibility. The idea that these are "optional extras" that can easily be discarded when tough choices are required just doesn't apply any more. This has been obvious from several major resource projects we've worked on in the last few years. For example, in many regions the loss or clearing of significant ecosystems must now be offset with newly established and protected habitat – and at a rate eight times the area lost. Requirements like these were just an aspiration of environmental regulators a decade ago. Now they're a legislated reality. This single example of the changing value boundary has major cost, resourcing and timing implications for organisations and it contributes to a very different value equation today.

This comes through very clearly when a company is undertaking multiple resource projects across a region or state. We recently worked with one business in this situation to help better understand the priority risks relating to its suite of mining projects.

Although the roles of participants ranged from strategy to operations the most critical issues were surprisingly relevant to all. Vegetation clearing and the need to establish acceptable and viable offsets emerged as major challenges across the company's operations. "*Our thinking needs to change on this*", said a senior project manager who had identified the problem. "*We've traditionally tried to solve these issues on a project-by-project basis but that isn't going to work – the problem is just too large and presents a real risk. We need a better solution that designs more strategic offsets on a regional and integrated program rather than trying to find site-by-site solutions. We can't afford not to take an integrated approach.*"

Planning for the closure of mining and other resource extraction sites is now starting to encompass factors well beyond the physical site boundary, which has traditionally been the focus of site decommissioning. Until recently, site remediation and rehabilitation of disturbed areas formed the basis for plans and costings. However, things have quickly and comprehensively changed.

An aluminium processing plant recently had its closure costs *doubled in just nine years* (to US$640 million) due to changing regulations about remediation of contaminated soil and sediments.

Mine closure is also increasingly not just about site remediation, but about restoring or establishing sequential land uses, and considering the role of the site, its infrastructure, workforce and local supply chain in the region's future development.

This wider set of factors involved in acceptable site closure has widened the focus from the site to the region, and from remediation to establishing valued land uses. What constitutes "greatest value" today is very different from a decade ago.

How the intangibles affect value

Anyone working in infrastructure design and delivery should have noticed the increasing trend across countries and cultures to hold project and infrastructure owners responsible for intangible costs rather than asking the community to bear this cost. For example, in 2011 the Deepwater Horizon oil spill in the Gulf of Mexico triggered more than 130 law suits and class actions against BP across a broad range of environmental damage and follow-on impacts, which some predict could extend over 20 years.

"Intangibles" typically refers to social and environmental issues and assets that are not traditionally assigned a market value, making them difficult to cost or assess their economic worth. Wetlands, significant ecosystems, cultural heritage and resilient communities have long been seen as important and worth protecting, but the significant shift to elevate their importance by assigning them monetary value has been driven by two factors. Firstly, their value is now recognised and appreciated by the community, and any erosion of their worth is a significant risk or constitutes an "unacceptable impact". Secondly, translating their value into quantifiable or monetary terms and rigorously building this into a project's financial analysis has given them a more visible role in financial assessments. Expanding the analysis to account for these externalities is becoming part of decision-making processes in many projects we work across. Including the externalities in project assessments along with all factors contributing to performance and effectiveness can change a project's scope, design and ultimately its value.

The CEO of a major public utility once told us, "*If we get a negative story on the front page of the newspaper, I cost that single event at $250,000. Don't ask me to state the science behind this. It's my gut feel. But the increase in community complaints, loss of trust, plus management and staff time dealing with the response, and greater political and regulatory scrutiny are all repercussions – and these have very real costs.*"

A landmark study to assess the worth of the World Heritage–listed Great Barrier Reef along the Australian coast yielded some surprising results. A 2009 study by the international consultancy Oxford Economics went beyond previous economic assessments of the reef, which had placed dollar figures just on the tourism, fishing and other commercial activities it supports. Oxford Economics also considered the many indirect (but vital) benefits of the reef, assessing its value at US$51.4 billion[3] – substantially more than previous assessments had calculated.

Indirect benefits the study identified revealed the reef's full value over the long term. These included its role in protecting coastal communities and infrastructure from severe storms as well as its capacity to yield previously undiscovered breakthroughs in biomedicines.

The key point is that the real value is a lot higher than conventional economics recognises. A useful way to think about this is to ask: "What would an annual insurance premium be to cover the true value of this asset?" While insurance may not be obtainable, it's a useful commercial construct to explore the way businesses might actually think about the value or cost to them of these non-market values.

Our view is that we must improve the methods and expertise we use, and get better at making realistic assumptions and intelligently applying surrogate or proxy measures. We can't just avoid this issue because it is difficult and challenging. Not to include these issues in economic or financial analyses makes them less visible, too easy to sideline or see as optional and only marginally important. They need to be mainstreamed into decisions.

Ecosystem services are a case in point. These services are the benefits we receive from the resources and processes supplied by natural ecosystems. They include clean drinking water, clean air, pollination of crops and breakdown of waste. While some assert that ecosystem services are priceless (because we literally can't live without them), others maintain that assessing their value is vital to fully appreciate their role and contribution.

In 2007, environment ministers from the governments of the G8+5 countries agreed to analyse the global economic benefit of biological diversity, and the cost of its loss or failure to take protective measures compared with the costs of effective conservation. The Work from TEEB[4] (The Economics of Ecosystems and Biodiversity) made a compelling economic case for conserving ecosystems and biodiversity, which has been picked up by the World Business Council on Sustainable Development. Just one example of this in practice – assessing the value of a coral reef system – demonstrates the logic.

3   Oxford Economics (2009) *Valuing the Effects of Great Barrier Reef Bleaching*, Great Barrier Reef Foundation, Brisbane

4   TEEB (2010) *The Economics of Ecosystems and Biodiversity. Mainstreaming the Economics of Nature: A synthesis of the approach, conclusions and recommendations of TEEB*, European Commission, Brussels

If you thought we'd never be able to "price nature" and cost the value of your favourite fishing spot or scenic rural landscapes, think again. Future projects will need to recognise the full worth of ecosystem services in their assessments of value.

But costing the intangibles doesn't just apply to the natural environment. We were involved in a recent United Kingdom study that calculated the economic value of well-designed streetscapes.[5] The community benefits were predictable in terms of safety, ease of navigation, lighting, reduced maintenance and amenity, but what also emerged was the clear *economic value* for others, including home owners, landlords, developers, local businesses and even local governments. The study highlighted the fact that it is possible to calculate the extra financial value of good street design over average or poor design. The study showed that improving street design quality can add, on average, over 5 per cent to residential prices and retail rents. This evidence-based approach helps build a solid business case to justify investment for good street design. It adds to the growing body of evidence refuting the myth that good design costs more – and demonstrates that return on investment is achieved in multiple ways.

5   CABE Space (2007) *Paved with gold: the real value of good street design*, Commission for Architecture and the Built Environment, London

Westpac Bank recently translated strategic risk into investment decisions by announcing its position of avoiding involvement in transactions "which support the establishment or long term continuation of inefficient and high carbon-emitting assets into the future."[6]

That statement comes after the banking sector was taken to task by Greenpeace for supporting fossil fuel projects. Similarly, HSBC states it will not provide financial services to activities in UNESCO World Heritage sites or internationally recognised wetlands, and will only invest in coal-fired power stations which have lower carbon intensities, with more robust standards for developed countries.[7]

The erosion of the value of coal-fired power stations in many countries reflects the chain of events described here. Changing community and political attitudes are translated into risk, which in turn influences how financial institutions assess long-term value.

The connection with supply chains

The experience of what happened to Gunns Limited and its pulp mill (in Chapter 2) also provides a good example of how pressures for sustainable operations are being transferred along supply chains. Customers, investors and interest groups are using their buying power and influence to change the product, service and operating characteristics of the supply chain from start to finish. Procurement and supply chain practices are now identified by many organisations as a key risk to their ongoing business.

Of course many developers, owners and operators of private and public infrastructure and facilities are responding. In 2001, Royal Dutch Shell cancelled 100 contracts with companies that failed to adhere to its ethical, health and safety, and environmental policies. More recently, it has embedded its expectations in a global Supplier Qualification System (SQS) designed to collect and store information about its current and prospective suppliers. The system requires providers to furnish information on finance, health and safety, quality management, insurance, products and services, corporate social responsibility (CSR) policies and legal information. This forms part of the internal process Shell uses to shortlist suppliers for purchasing activities. It serves as a register of suppliers worldwide and ensures that supplier profiles are visible to the Shell global organisation.

6 Westpac Bank (2012) *Financing Sustainable Energy Position Statement*, http://www.westpac.com.au/docs/pdf/aw/Position_statement_on_sustainable_energy.pdf

7 http://www.hsbc.com/citizenship/sustainability/sustainability-risk/equator-principles-and-sector-policies

Investors are paying attention

Today's investors are acutely aware of and sensitised to a wider spectrum of risks to return on their investments. They want more evidence that the organisations they're investing in are operating ethically and are effectively managing their short and longer-term risks.

Ratings analysts are reflecting this growing interest, placing greater weight on sustainability aspects in their evaluation of companies. The changes stem partly from a realisation by institutional investors that climate change and sustainability issues often bear directly on the risk profiles of companies, their reputations and their financial performance. Equity analysts have begun to consider the sustainability practices of the companies they cover. Bloomberg, Standard & Poors, Moody, Thomson Reuters and Goldman Sachs now provide corporate ESG (environment, societal and governance) information such as emissions data, figures on energy consumption, corporate policies and board composition. That information was kept hidden or shared sparingly until quite recently – but now it's online and available to all.

There are also more specialised providers of sustainability ratings like the Dow Jones Sustainability Indexes, the Carbon Disclosure Leadership Index, the FTSE4Good Index Series and the NASDAQ OMX CRD Global Sustainability Index.

Insurers are also paying attention

Insurers are keenly aware of social and environmental risks. Claims arising from natural disasters are escalating and present a real threat to the insurance industry. Insurers may be unable or unwilling to cover these hazards in future as natural disasters cost the global insurance industry around US$110 billion in 2011. For many insurers, the weather-related risk has become so high they have stopped writing flood insurance. The cost of Hurricane Sandy on the east coast of the United States in 2012 is estimated at up to US$50 billion (compared with the cost of Hurricane Katrina at US$100 billion in 2005), and private insurance is expected to cover only US$20 billion of this amount.

Take the example

Another example is the situation of a major coal mine in Australia. After a cyclone caused flooding in 2010, it cost the operating company millions of dollars to refurbish damaged draglines in the mine, with months of lost production.

The company's London insurer insisted it upgrade its flood protection from a 1 in 20–year flood to a 1 in 1000–year event. In effect, the coal mine became self-insuring against the damages of floods.

The insured losses associated with natural and man-made catastrophes continue to rise.[8] The losses, which seem to be growing exponentially, are not just a function of more frequent extreme events. They are also due to increasing urbanisation – the areas being impacted are bigger and more populous, with more assets being damaged or destroyed.

Insured natural and man-made catastrophe losses 1970-2011 (US$B at 2011 prices)

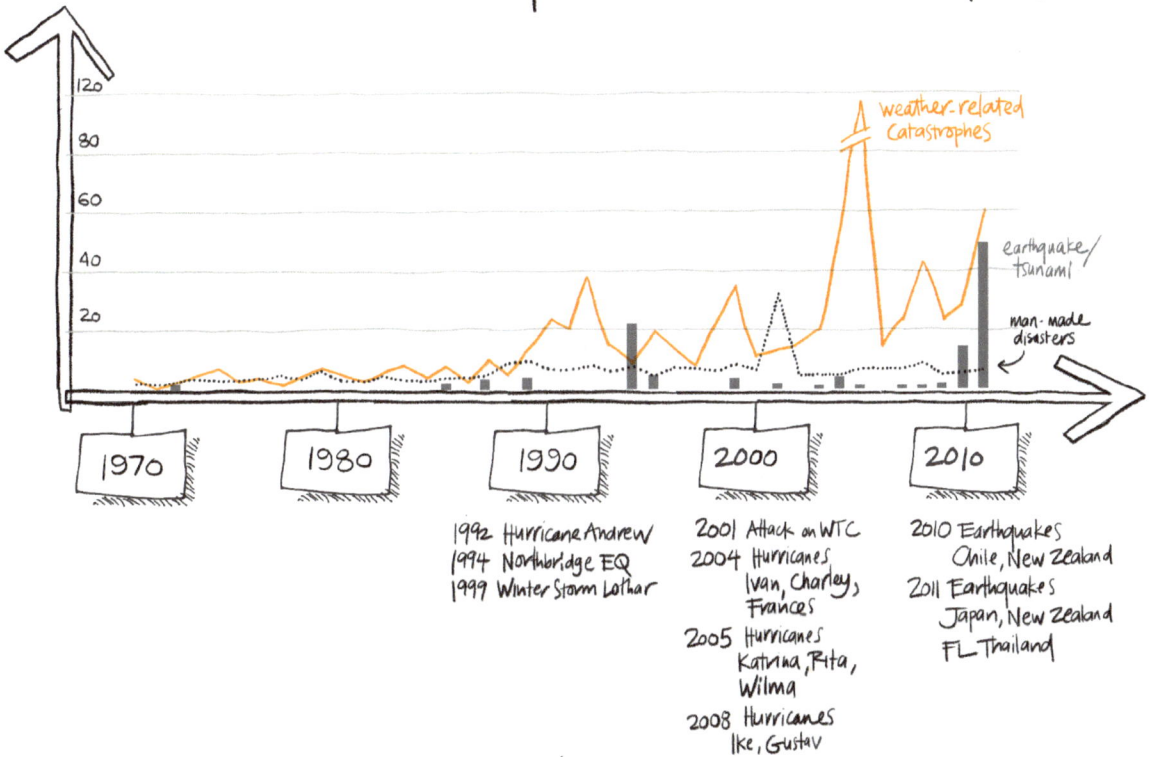

weather-related catastrophes

earthquake/tsunami

man-made disasters

| 120 |
| 80 |
| 60 |
| 40 |
| 20 |

1970   1980   1990   2000   2010

1992 Hurricane Andrew
1994 Northbridge EQ
1999 Winter Storm Lothar

2001 Attack on WTC
2004 Hurricanes Ivan, Charley, Frances
2005 Hurricanes Katrina, Rita, Wilma
2008 Hurricanes Ike, Gustav

2010 Earthquakes Chile, New Zealand
2011 Earthquakes Japan, New Zealand FL Thailand

8   Swiss Re (2012) *Flood – an underestimated risk*, Swiss Reinsurance Company Ltd, Zurich

50% of companies report sustainability initiatives will improve their bottom line

Does sustainability pay off financially?

While there are financial risks to avoid in sustainability, there are also financial rewards to reap from a more sustainable approach and practices.

This is borne out in a 2013 study by Boston Consulting Group, which showed that participating companies reporting a profit from their sustainability efforts rose 23 percent from that of the previous year.[9] The study, involving 2,600 executives and managers, also found nearly half said their companies had changed its business model as a result of sustainability opportunities. Interestingly, their perspective is one of building a competitive advantage through innovation, rather than seeing it as a cost issue.

The argument here is not that sustainability measures are *the* reason for high performance in companies, although they do contribute. Rather it is the high-performing organisations with strong leadership that embrace sustainability issues and opportunities. These companies exhibit common characteristics including a focus on long-term strategy (not just short-term gains), strong corporate governance, sound risk-management practices, and a history of investment in green innovations.[10]

The message is clear: understand and assess value from a broad and informed perspective – or be penalised later by more stringent and comprehensive requirements. Delaying action will very likely require mitigation, correction, retrofitting, upgrading, redesign or even relocation in future, with all the accompanying delays, disruption and cost.

We see those who adopt a broader approach to risk and value deal better with uncertainty, and are less reactive to change because they anticipate it. The risks and costs of inaction, of working within an overly narrow scope, or assuming critical parameters will not change over a project's lifetime are increasing. Astute business and project decisions will increasingly demand more holistic assessments of value and risk.

This changing value equation does not, however, necessarily mean higher costs, a lower return on investment or applying expensive and complex technologies. It's not just a matter of waiting for the right technologies to solve all our problems, either. We explore this aspect in the next chapter.

9   MIT Sloan and the Boston Consulting Group (2013) *The Innovation Bottom Line*, MIT Sloan Management Review, Cambridge MA

10 A.T. Kearney (2009) *Green winners: the performance of sustainability-focused companies during the financial crisis*, Chicago.
http://www.atkearney.com/documents/10192/6972076a-9cdc-4b20-bc3a-d2a4c43c9c21

USEFUL QUESTIONS

- What is a government or community going to define as an "acceptable impact" in 5 or 10 years? How does this affect the assumptions underpinning a project's value?

- Are the intangibles or externalities fully understood? How are they included in a project's financial assessments?

- What is the position on sustainable development of those funding the projects, and what are their requirements?

- Have the material whole-of-life risks to your assets been accurately assessed and represented on your organisation's balance sheet?

Four

Technology is just part of the answer

Sustainable solutions can be achieved in technologically simple ways.

Elegant simplicity is a powerful design goal.

A proactive, purposeful process of design is crucial.

"The technologies which have had the most profound effects on human life are usually simple."

Freeman Dyson,
renowned theoretical physicist and mathematician[11]

11 *Infinite in All Directions*, (2004) Harper Perennial

Technology is an integral part of our modern world. It has a profound effect on our lives – the way we communicate, travel, undertake our work, live in and equip our homes, and maintain our health. Indeed, our ability to develop and deploy technology is one of the characteristics that make humans a unique and dominant species on Earth.

The introduction of steam-power technology enabled printing presses to operate at much greater speed and lower cost. Books and newspapers proliferated in Europe and America, fostering a dramatic growth in literacy and a better-educated workforce that could handle the more complicated operations of a coal-powered, steam-driven rail and factory economy. This one key item of technology triggered the First Industrial Revolution.

A second technological development in the first decade of the 1900s – electrical communication – converged with oil-powered combustion engines to give rise to the Second Industrial Revolution. Electrified factories could achieve even greater scales of production, including mass production of vehicles that would entirely alter the spatial and temporal scales of agriculture and society within a generation.

From simple aircraft to space travel, posted mail to the internet, and basic brewing to modern genetic engineering, the world has ridden the wave of an inter-connected technology explosion. Throughout the 20th century, the growing scale and efficiency of resource extraction and manufacturing enabled a 20-fold increase in global economic output while the price of raw materials reduced by half in real terms.[12] Developed nations took greatest advantage, supporting growth in health, wealth and living standards.

Now in the 21st century, where is technology taking us? Is technology the solution to the sustainability challenge? Perhaps more importantly, *how should we think about technology and the choices we face in its design, selection and use?*

---

12 McKinsey (2011) *Resource revolution: meeting the world's energy, materials, food and water needs,* McKinsey Global Institute. http://www.mckinsey.com/features/resource_revolution

Fostering an industrial revolution

The world's rapidly growing population drives escalating pollution and resource pressures that demand attention. The kind of resource-intensive production processes that are commonplace today in developed countries cannot be replicated in developing countries without causing catastrophic environmental harm and social disruption. Thus, delivery of security, health and wellbeing to a majority of the global population demands dramatic improvements in the productive capacity of natural and human systems.

Indeed, the decline in resource prices achieved over the past century has been entirely reversed within the last decade. The rapidly growing middle class in developing countries has driven up demand, increasing the price of resources that are also increasingly difficult and expensive to obtain (such as oil, and rare earth minerals used in electronics). Tightening environmental regulations and social expectations have concurrently raised the bar on development practices, translating into further price rises.

So it's clear that some conventional technologies have greatly diminishing value to our global future. Cleaner technologies that enable order-of-magnitude improvements in resource productivity are required.

Of course, the limits to development are not absolute despite the finite carrying capacity of natural ecosystems. Rather, they are determined by the effectiveness of technology and social organisation.

Throughout history, economic transformations have occurred when a new communication technology has converged with and provided the medium for organising around new energy systems. These transformations have enhanced economic prosperity, providing the conditions in which people feel most able to care for their communities and environment. Yet wealth and poverty can be equally destructive. Under the prevailing set of Western values and technologies, wealth enables massive resource consumption. Poverty typically drives exploitation of natural resources and destruction of the environment. Again, this reinforces the requirement for clean forms of development and high levels of resource efficiency that support growing standards of living, particularly in emerging economies.

So, individually and collectively, we have a choice. In our capacity as voters, customers, business leaders and government officials we can apply economic instruments, legislative measures and consumer demand to shape the development and use of technology.

Which technologies will be supported, and which abandoned? There's a strong argument to favour technologies that enable decoupling of economic growth and development from consumption of natural resources and generation of waste.

Furthermore, while efficiency gains (the focus of much new technology development to produce more from less, faster) can and must contribute to the improvement of productive capacity alongside resource conservation, new technologies will undoubtedly be required. Industries will develop around base-load renewable energy, carbon capture and storage, and water reclamation, while out-dated technologies are retired. Indeed, if we are to achieve our societal aspirations for the future, whole industries will necessarily undergo structural reform, just as they have in the past. It's the transition that is fuelling growth in companies like GE and Unilever as well as clean-tech start-ups like Opower and NovaLED.

Will this trend continue? Is it the next industrial revolution arising from the confluence of internet communication with the efficient generation, storage, distribution and use of renewable energy? Is this the techno-fix we need?

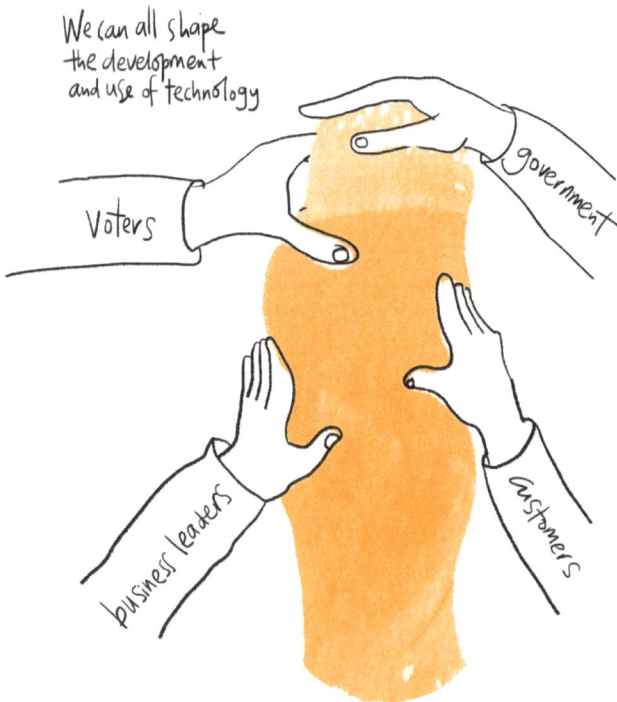

We can all shape the development and use of technology

Voters

government

business leaders

customers

Taking big steps with existing technology

Working for an organisation that trades on its knowledge and application of leading technologies, it would be easy to devote attention to clean technologies and their likely implications for business and industry. But we won't, because while technological change and innovation are no doubt important to sustainable development, we argue against succumbing to the illusion or even the necessity of a "techno-fix".

Take carbon capture and storage, which is regarded as a key part of the technological solution to human-induced climate change. Carbon storage is about extracting and then sequestering carbon from the atmosphere in underground reservoirs. While aspects of the technology required are proven, other aspects are still in development and may be 10 to 20 years away from widespread commercial application.[13] In the meantime, we simply need other ways to dramatically reduce greenhouse gas emissions to avoid the worst impacts of climate change. We can't wait idly by.

Fortunately, much can be achieved with existing technology.

The growing waste challenge offers an example. Not only are countries like the United Kingdom facing rapidly increasing disposal costs, there are also great opportunities to recover and transform the waste into resources, creating jobs and economic activity in the process.

The technology already exists. Instead the task is reorienting taxes, subsidies and regulations against pollution and waste and in favour of resource recovery. Substantial progress in this direction has been made in the past few years with the aim of taking England toward a zero waste economy. Over 40 per cent of household waste was recycled in England in 2010/11, compared with 11 per cent in 2000/01. Over half (52 per cent) of England's commercial and industrial waste was recycled or reused in 2009, compared with 42 per cent in 2002/03.[14]

There are also project-level situations where simple technologies can deliver more sustainable outcomes.

We see this repeatedly across our work with organisations, particularly those developing large infrastructure assets. Often the response to project challenges and impacts is to "bolt on" features to make corrections or mitigate problems, without standing back to consider the resulting configuration, complexity and consequences. While it can take a little extra thought and effort, reducing complexity delivers more streamlined and simple solutions that invariably contribute to sustainable development by reducing associated social, environmental and business risks, resource consumption and making more productive use of the available capital. Indeed, what's interesting is that an apparent paradox seems to be emerging – rising technological sophistication is occurring at the same time as a trend towards adaptability and simplification of technology solutions.

13 http://cdn.globalccsinstitute.com/sites/default/files/publications/56466/factbook-bringing-carbon-capture-storage-market.pdf

14 http://www.defra.gov.uk/environment/waste/

Take the example We worked with a project team developing a new and significant copper mine in south-east Asia. A pipeline had been selected as the method of transporting copper slurry from the new mine to a coastal port 400 km away. A road would be built alongside for construction and maintenance purposes. But when examined in its wider context, some unforeseen problems emerged. The heavily forested terrain experienced regular earthquakes and intense rainfall, presenting maintenance problems. The road would open the land to piecemeal development and clearing of significant rainforest, and thousands of people were likely to migrate to the area using the road in search of work, "camping out" in the vicinity of the mine with few resources and few prospects.

The potential for unrest, disease and impacts on nearby villages was high. In short, a technology that worked well in other situations was inappropriate. So the team went back to basics: the primary goal was transporting copper slurry to port. An alternative solution did exist – using river barges. This solution avoided the risks linked with the pipeline, and created benefits including employment of local villagers (looking for benefits from the mine) who had impressive river navigation and boat handling skills. This simpler solution eliminated some key social and environmental risks, created direct and flow-on community benefits, and enhanced the mine's social licence to operate. It was a *simple and appropriate* technology solution for its context – far beyond a merely efficient solution.

Pursuing simplicity

We find that when risk assessments are conducted on planned infrastructure assets and take into consideration a realistic spectrum of risks (and their interdependencies) over the planned life of the infrastructure asset, one thing becomes starkly clear – that beyond the short term, the operating conditions and requirements for the asset are often highly uncertain. The error bands around predicted future events (such as traffic forecasts, or industrial demand for water or energy) are substantial, eroding confidence that current designs are also "fit for the future".

Climate change projections raise further considerable uncertainty about the nature of the future operating environment, and this means adaptable designs are simply good sense.

We also consistently observe that a focus in infrastructure design on "de-risking" – that is, elimination of risk rather than mitigation of risk – often leads to more simple and elegant designs using existing technologies, even within complex, highly regulated operating environments.

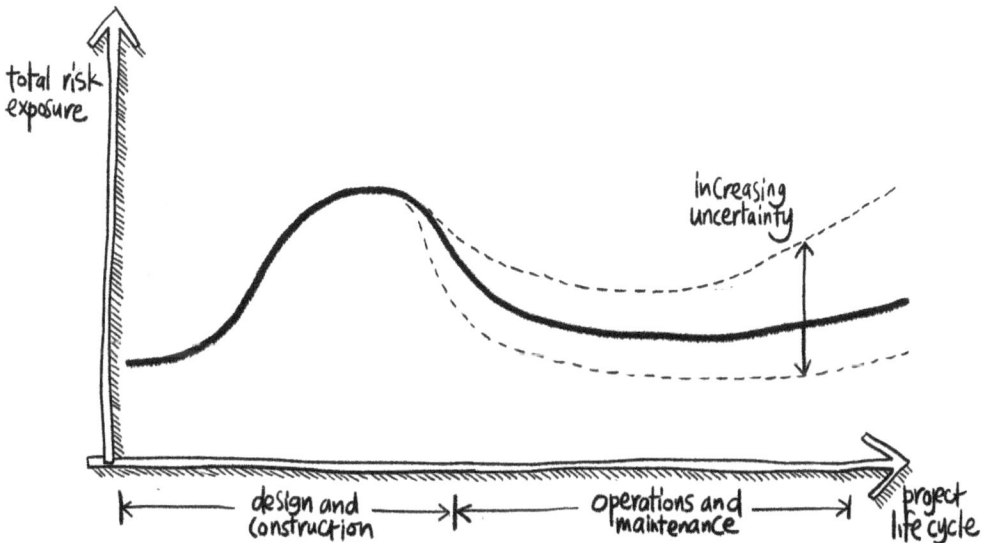

Simplest Solution?
Move the School.

Take the example

A major highway realignment was occurring close to a school. "The school mustn't be impacted in any way, and I'll be paying close attention to the environmental clean-up and revegetation activities. No health or environmental risks are acceptable," was the clear message from the regulator involved. These requirements had translated into a design involving a long bridge costing US$40 million to skirt the school grounds, along with extensive landscaping and revegetation. "Somehow this solution seems over-baked. Isn't there a much simpler solution?" we asked. Stepping back from the task of designing and building a road bridge to look at the bigger picture, the delivery team started to imagine different solutions. A contractor asked "Can we move the school?"

When the laughter abated, it appeared this was not such a silly question. The delivery team had assumed "no impact" on the school ruled this out, but in fact that assumption hadn't been tested. Even the authorities scoffed when the idea was raised, but when pressed further conceded it could theoretically be feasible. What happened? The delivery team identified an alternative school site very close by, and a new, modern school was built incorporating an environmental awareness space. The bridge was then substantially shortened and environmental works reduced accordingly. Even including the cost of the new school, the overall project cost was reduced by US$10 million.

Significantly, there can be major benefits for infrastructure developers and operators from simpler, more adaptable designs. The benefits come by way of reduced up-front capital costs, deferred or avoided capacity augmentation costs, and lower operating costs. At a time when governments around the world are under enormous fiscal pressure that is likely to be sustained, and depressed economies are putting similar pressure on private enterprise, these types of substantial cost saving opportunities are not to be overlooked.

Smart design provides the potential for a simpler infrastructure product with many flow-on benefits, including lower resource consumption, less stakeholder opposition, faster approvals, lower capital and operating costs (capex and opex) and greater resilience. This means starting at the core of the problem, rather than taking a "business as usual" (BAU) solution and then tacking on additions.

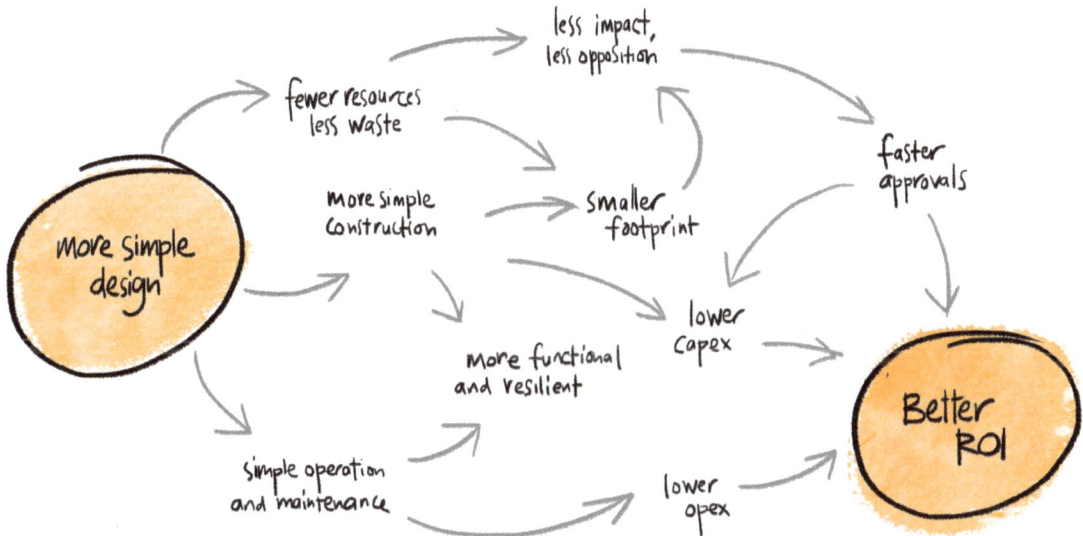

Furthermore, technologically-advanced and integrated infrastructure systems do carry risks. When failures occur (as with the inter-linked global economy) systems can unravel in expansive and surprising ways. The interdependencies that exist today in cities in developed countries are manyfold. Power generation depends on water systems for cooling, while water systems depend on energy for pumping and treatment. Transport systems depend on power for lighting, traffic controls and movement of people and freight, including the food that gets delivered "just in time" to supermarkets. Even our ability to get cash depends on power reaching automatic teller machines.

Our experience is telling us that elegant simplicity (not frugality) is a powerful design goal that has been overlooked. It should be revisited.

The process of designing a sustainable future

Perhaps contrary to popular perception, we believe the adequacy of technology is invariably not the barrier to scoping and implementing effective, sustainable infrastructure solutions. Nor is the substantial inertia that exists in long-lived infrastructure and institutions. Rather, social, economic, political and institutional factors characterise much of the inherent complexity, all underpinned by human factors and frailties. Effective communication to develop understanding, build shared interests, and find mutually acceptable solutions and transformation pathways is the key factor in achieving progress and success.

So while new technologies are important for sustainable development, their lack is not a barrier to significant progress. Instead, the *process* of design is as important as – if not more important – than the content of design (i.e. technology). Indeed, our desire to enhance the process of design is a key motivation for this book. We devote several of the chapters that follow to this aspect.

Many people don't realise just how fragile
our increasingly high-tech cities can be –
although people and communities that have
experienced extreme floods and storms in
recent years have tragic insight into their
effects. Natural or man-made disasters can
wreak havoc on the inter-connected systems
that provide the macro-fabric for our society,
with massive repair bills over long periods.
This brings into question the whole aspect of
the longer-term resilience and affordability of
our city and regional infrastructure, both for
owners and operators and for the residents
and users of those assets.

Selecting the appropriate technology

A more useful way of approaching the role of technology in sustainable development is to ask "what is appropriate technology in this situation?" In a similar vein, it is useful to think about designing infrastructure assets that are "fit for purpose". In both instances, fit and appropriate solutions are a function of the social, political, legal, economic, environmental and technological context they are created in, along with the needs of users, and how these evolve over time.

When the idea of appropriate, "fit for purpose" solutions is combined with notions of technology adaptability and design simplification, it signals that the design, development and operation of sustainable, resilient and affordable infrastructure must be strategically informed. A wider systemic view must be taken of the operating context for an infrastructure asset over its life, the risks and conditions it will face, and the objectives for which it is being established. The design process and specification of parameters to evaluate the merit of designs are crucial.

With respect to technology selection and deployment, the task then is to adjust the prevailing emphasis on new technology and resource efficiency improvement. Rather than being passive receptors of technology, we can and should be proactive, purposeful determinants of its form and application, expanding our view to design simplification, asset de-risking and solutions that are appropriate as well as adaptable over their design lives.

This is where we now focus much of the following discussion in this book.

USEFUL QUESTIONS

- Are we at risk of using conventional technologies because it's the easy thing to do rather than being a considered decision?

- What technology choices will still seem like smart choices in 5, 10 and 20 years?

- Is the chosen design and technology mix resilient in the face of a changing operating environment and connected infrastructure systems?

Five

Setting the path to success

An ambitious goal can be the key to unlock powerful solutions.

Set a clear goal or design intent.

Commit to achieving it.

"The most effective way to
manage change is to create it..."

Peter Drucker, management consultant[15]

15 "A Survey of the Near Future: the Next Society", *The Economist*, November 2001

How do we make our 30-year-old treatment plant a sustainable asset?

Corporate sustainability strategy

FACT
⇑ energy $

FACT
methane gas

FACT
biosolid waste

SOLUTION
⇑ earnings by using buffer zone around plant

SOLUTION
harvest for energy

SOLUTION
manufacture agricultural fertiliser

Consulting to organisations on sustainability for many years now, we've developed ways of cultivating real understanding of its connection to their core business. Our conversations can ignite ideas that generate valuable new projects and results not thought possible.

Take the example

Take the example of three executives in the water industry we first met several years ago. Within their portfolio of responsibilities was the management of a 30-year-old wastewater treatment plant. The executives shared the company's view that it was largely a liability. The plant had high energy costs, produced methane that caused odours the community complained about, and generated biosolid waste that required careful management and disposal.

The executives later admitted that when they arrived at our workshop to explore ways in which a sustainable approach to business might add value, they thought sustainability was just a "green fringe issue" with little bearing on their water plant. After our workshop, one approached us. *"This is the first time someone got me involved in a good practical discussion about sustainability and how it relates to our assets,"* he said. *"You've got me thinking…there's some opportunities I want to explore!"* Talking to his colleagues as they returned to the office, they agreed the workshop had changed their thinking about what it would take to sustain business success in future.

One posed the question: *"How can we make our wastewater treatment plant a sustainable asset?"* Over the following days the executives continued their conversation: *"Could we use the methane to generate some of the plant's energy? Could we convert the biosolids to agricultural fertiliser and sell it? Could we make better use of the land operating as a buffer zone around the plant?"* They devoted time over the next months to find viable answers to these questions.

Within two years, the executives had transformed their treatment plant from a liability into a valuable asset. They co-located and partnered with other businesses to create an energy and resource recovery precinct, which now generates income and has boosted local employment. The environmental impacts of the plant were substantially reduced. Their activities strengthened the company's reputation with industry peers, regulators and the community, and they were recognised in several leading industry awards. All this from a simple intentional question about making operations more sustainable.

What's your design intent?

American architect and designer William McDonough is prominent in his field for challenging how we make things. In his best-selling 2002 book, *Cradle to Cradle: Remaking the Way We Make Things*, he asked why today's designers work to merely *minimise* possible negative impacts of the things they create, when they have all the tools and resources to *eliminate* them.

McDonough and his co-author, German chemist Michael Braungart, set out a convincing argument using evidence and examples to show it's entirely possible for growth and development to generate only *positive* financial, social and ecological results, for everyone.

The philosophy behind McDonough's argument is that "design is the first expression of intention". At first, this seems an obvious statement, but McDonough has articulated a powerful concept that warrants more attention.

Without consciously realising it, people often set business or project objectives that are unclear, narrow and short-sighted. Sometimes we avoid stretching our goals or thinking about new ways to achieve them because we think it will take more effort, time and risk; so conservative responses masquerade as pragmatism. When we're discussing new options with project managers it's not uncommon to hear: "*We know what we need to do. There's a right and wrong way to do this. We've done it before and know what works, so don't go wasting time looking for new solutions.*" These views can be reinforced by design and practice standards and disciplinary stubbornness that entrench the status quo.

Probing "intent" a little more deeply

When we apply this idea of *design intent* to the various projects we work on, we often reveal hidden assumptions and misplaced optimism.

Let's say for example, we apply the thinking of design intent to the development of a new mine in a developing economy. The company expects to earn substantial income from the metals it extracts over 20 years. The mine will make a substantial contribution to the national and local economies and will create hundreds of jobs. The mining activities will also generate acidic drainage water with the potential to pollute and destroy the local environment (for a generation at least) but the company will manage this (at considerable cost) during the mine's lifespan.

The engineers, the company's executives and its Board members all accept with optimism that the acid drainage will always be well managed – but nobody can predict the future and say this is certain. So, by accepting the generation of acid drainage, the *intent* of the engineers, executives and the Board is to impose a pollution risk on the landscape and surrounding community, as well as an enduring liability that might damage the company's profitability and standing with investors, regulators and other groups important to its success.

Perhaps this risk could be avoided if someone at the start of the project asked, "Is this *really* our design intent? Will or should our shareholders really accept a risk like this? Is our Board happy to risk their careers and reputation? Is it acceptable for people to live with a potential environmental catastrophe in their local area?" We doubt the engineers, the executives or the Board of this mining company would say "yes" to these questions other than for reasons of "pragmatism".

Without determination, it's just talk

Perhaps the intent of the company could be expressed differently from the way the design team put it, as: "How can we extract the metals profitably without any environmental and business legacy from acid drainage?"

When questions like these are posed to project teams we usually hear a few standard early responses: "It's easy to put out that challenge, but it's just not realistic to achieve," or "There's nothing new in that challenge. We've been working to reduce the impact of our operations for years!" These are dismissive and defensive statements. They presume new solutions aren't possible and that we can't design and shape our future to generate predominantly positive outcomes, when in fact we can – if that's what we set out to achieve.

There are two dimensions of intent – the clarity of *purpose* and the *determination* to fulfil that purpose. The organisations we work with have everything they need to create new, smarter and more valuable solutions – but only if their objective or intent is clear, and if they are determined to establish *how* to achieve that objective.

You get what you ask for

"What does the perfect port look like?" This was the question we posed to a group of 25 experts from diverse disciplines charged with planning an expanded port facility for a global mining company.

We gave each expert 10 minutes to sketch an image of "their perfect port". Each person then shared a key feature of their port with the group. Each sketched out different ideas but they all shared a common element – not a single picture matched what they expected to build! It showed that everyone felt the expected solution could be improved. One participant observed: "If we consolidate everyone's ideas then I suppose we're really all talking about a more sustainable port". So "the perfect port" had become a "sustainable port".

This short exercise demonstrated that the *possibility as well as the desire* existed in the project team to design a better port facility – but it only happened when team members were asked to do that. The simple question, *What's the perfect port?* had expanded the design objectives and the creative space for this group of professionals. We've seen this situation play out time and again. Most people want to be part of something new and better. The opportunity to get involved in solving a challenging problem is what motivates them. If you set a clear intent, you'll find everyone contributes something worthwhile.

However, we often underestimate our ability to develop practical and innovative solutions. How often do you filter out new ideas you might have, assuming your colleagues or customers won't be interested? How often do we send a signal of lack of interest to others?

If you set a clear intent and commit to generating new thinking in your organisation, it's likely you'll achieve that intent. We find questions that start with "how" are important: *How can we upgrade this plant to extend its operating life while substantially reducing its energy costs? How can we enhance the prosperity of irrigation communities while halving their water use? How can we increase our revenue 25 per cent while cutting our raw material use by the same measure?* The questions you ask – and the people you ask – are important (and we'll talk about this more later).

Unilever, one of the world's biggest food and beverage companies, tapped into the passion and insights of a global audience to "crowd-source" solutions to its business challenges related to sustainable sourcing, production and distribution.

In just 24 hours, over 2,200 registrants from 77 countries posted almost 4,000 comments, many of them insightful and full of possibilities. The company is now investigating and acting upon them.

- eliminate or cover the ore stockpiles
- no people involved in ship mooring
- use gravity for ore delivery and movement
- increase ore moisture at the mine, not the port

- make the facility visually interesting
- no increase in dust for local communities
- make it a place people visit to learn about mining

- dramatically reduced water usage
- no dredging
- no encroachment on the coast and turtle habitat

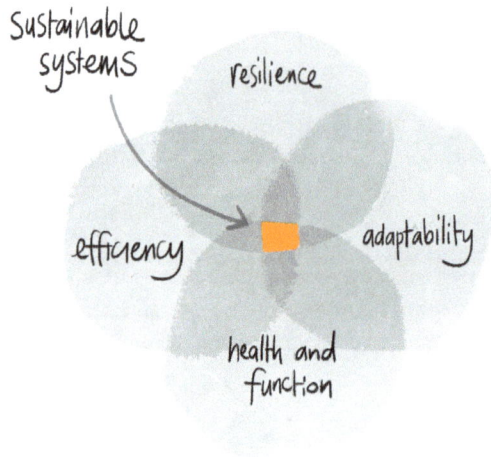

Sustainable
systems

resilience

efficiency

adaptability

health and
function

What should we be designing for?

So, what should we be "designing" for?
What are the characteristics of a useful,
sustainable design?

There's no lack of information on sustainability.
Google "sustainability definition" or
"sustainability objectives" and over 20
million results appear. They vary in their form
and focus but common features include an
interest in achieving the lowest whole-of-life
cost to design, construct and operate, while
contributing to vibrant and strong communities
where the benefits of development are shared
equally and the natural environment
is protected.

While these are useful pointers to the intent of
sustainable design, we think another important
concept needs highlighting – the importance
of building *viable and resilient systems*.

We believe there are four core attributes
of such systems:

- **Resilience** – the capacity to recover
  from dramatic shocks.

- **Adaptability** – the capacity to evolve
  with longer term change.

- **Health and function** – involving
  maintenance of the integrity of systems
  so they continue to function well.

- **Efficiency** – so resources are used
  sparingly and waste is avoided.

These attributes can be usefully applied
to complex systems such as infrastructure
networks, natural ecosystems and even
national economies.

Take the example
An easy example is available: the often overlooked but important stormwater drainage systems serving urban landscapes. How might the system attributes listed above apply to an urban drainage system to improve its cost effectiveness, resilience, health and sustainability?

Here are just a few ways:

1) Vehicle accidents and spills present risks of "peak loads" of pollutants entering the drainage network. With changing climates and more extreme storm events, the "first flush" of pollutants from road surfaces becomes more pronounced. To be resilient to these shocks, the stormwater network could include detention ponds to detain pollutants for safe removal.

2) The performance expectations of urban drainage networks can also change as urban areas are developed and water runoff increases, while changes in climate can compound the "heat island" effect in cities. Growing demand and limited availability make water more valuable. So to be adaptive, the drainage network could include more natural overland flow paths to accommodate higher flows that also provide green open space to enhance urban amenity and cooling.

3) Stormwater drainage systems are part of a wider network of catchment drainage. Piped systems typically discharge into rivers and estuaries and high pollutant loads or flows causing erosion can compromise the overall system health and function. Adverse reactions from the community and regulators can mean unplanned, costly corrections to the stormwater drainage network. Managing flows and pollutants from the outset helps ensure the overall health, function and cost effectiveness of the entire system.

4) Urban drainage networks are designed to operate efficiently, removing water from roads and properties to minimise flood risk. These systems also need to be maintained or upgraded and kept clear of litter and other debris. The whole-of-life operating cost efficiency is an important consideration. Integrating drainage safely into open, landscaped drainage paths will simplify maintenance and enhance adjacent property values, generating flow-on benefits to revenue streams from higher land tax income.

Why are these sustainable system attributes important? It's because we have imperfect knowledge, institutions and systems for management. We can't know or implement the "right" or perfect solutions. The global financial crisis reminded us how quickly complex, interconnected systems can unravel when the core system attributes are not maintained. So we should not naively or arrogantly "pick instant winners" assuming we have the right or perfect design for the solutions we need. Rather, our design intent should be informed by the aim of maintaining viable, productive and resilient systems with the capacity to evolve in response to changing knowledge, needs and conditions.

Sustainability $\neq$ time + money

One of the most inhibitive myths we hear about sustainable development is that it always means "more time and money". There are reasons why this can be the case, but it is not the rule.

The sustainable pay-off

Consider embarking on a planning and design process with the express intent of achieving a better solution at equal or less cost. Our experience reveals it is often possible to conceive solutions that cost less as well as delivering substantially greater value over their design life *if this is a stated objective and the problem solvers are given the latitude to explore alternative solutions.* You will see this illustrated in a variety of ways throughout this book, but a couple of observations for now include:

- Sustainable design often leads to simplification of design (as we introduced in Chapter 4) – this reduces the scale of construction impact and operational resource requirements, which in turn reduces capital and operating costs.

- Investing in smarter solutions at the front end of major infrastructure projects is a small percentage of the total cost – the cost savings of designing for better long-term outcomes can repay the initial investment many times over.

- Whole-of-life costing shows substantial operating savings are possible with sustainable design – this more than offsets occasions where the up-front capital cost is higher than traditional solutions.

Let's return to the port project. Just a few days after we asked what the perfect port looked like, the design team conceived a new and practical solution to largely eliminate any environmental impacts (on coastal and marine communities) and social impacts (noise and dust on local communities). This involved simplifying the overall design, which generated massive savings in materials, energy and operating and maintenance requirements. The cost of the design process to achieve this was conservatively estimated at US$0.2 million. The possible savings generated were in the order of tens of millions of dollars.

Truly sustainable design.

So in summary, project and business solutions reflect our intent – consciously or otherwise. Their achievement should not be limited by shallow thought or passive resignation – instead, they can be accelerated by incisive thought and deliberate action. The calibre of our questioning is a core determinant of what is possible. Read on.

USEFUL QUESTIONS

The decisions we make today have an ongoing effect, particularly when they involve long-lived physical infrastructure that shapes our regions, cities and society. Purposeful action or passive inaction will shape our future.
The critical questions are:

- What is the preferred future we are working towards?

- What is our specific design intent?

- How will we define and measure the success of our design intent?

- Have we informed and equipped people to pursue the intent without unreasonable constraints?

Six

Using the power of questions

Good questions get everyone involved.

Spend time working out what questions really matter.

Powerful questions provide new insights, ideas and solutions.

"Judge a man by his questions
rather than his answers."

Voltaire (François-Marie Arouet),
French Enlightenment writer,
historian and philosopher[16]

16 http://www.brainyquote.com/quotes/quotes/v/voltaire100338.html

The questions we ask determine the answers we get.

We need to put our effort, investment and ingenuity into the problems that really matter. Determining what those problems are is a function of our ability to ask probing, insightful questions – powerful questions. And yet the very questions that trigger and shape much of the work we do are rarely highlighted as important.

Within action-oriented cultures that thrive on production and achievement, fierce corporate and political debates can ensue over who has the "right" or "best" answer. But when did you last hear someone being recognised for having a great question? What questions do you ask in your daily work? How often do you ask questions that go beyond what's simply needed to get a particular task done? How do you even know if you're asking an important or powerful question?

We've thought of the importance of questions more than a few times as successive Australian governments have worked to restore the health of the nation's Murray–Darling Basin. This inland Basin occupies 14 per cent of the continent's land mass and produces a third of Australia's food, much of it coming from irrigated farms. Settlement and development have placed considerable pressure on the natural environment, threatening the ecological values of the Basin and its vital agricultural, tourism and related industries. Over the last decade, governments have invested billions of dollars to recover water from irrigated agriculture to keep it in the Basin's river systems, particularly for maintaining its high-value ecological assets. Irrigated agricultural land has been purchased and retired, and new infrastructure constructed to improve the efficiency of water delivery and use. Yet people remain dissatisfied. A revised Murray-Darling Basin Plan released in late 2012 called for a further 2,750 gigalitres of water for the environment. Everyone found fault with it – the scientists, the farmers, the state governments and the rural communities.

We wonder if the way this challenge is framed creates a barrier to developing solutions that everybody supports. Standing back from the detail of the debate, the central question that seems to drive governments in developing their solutions for the Murray–Darling Basin is: *How can we recover water for the environment with minimal impact on irrigation communities?* Perhaps a more useful question is: *How can we improve the prosperity and resilience of regional communities so they contribute to world food security despite less water being available for irrigation?*

Framed this way, might people work together on the challenge, rather than taking opposing sides?

What makes a great question?

Our work usually involves challenging the status quo, so we've become keenly interested in how to ask questions to build agreement and action for change.

We like the approach and work of Eric Vogt, a renowned American strategic consultant and innovative educator with an interest in "powerful questions". Vogt and his colleagues researched the use of questions within professions and across cultures, presenting their insights in the book, *The Art of Powerful Questions*.[17] They concluded that powerful questions share common traits – they stimulate reflective conversation and challenge underlying assumptions, and they "travel well" to connect networks of people, generating curiosity and inviting creativity as well as prompting new questions and opening new possibilities. A powerful question channels attention and energy and connects with deeper meaning and aspirations.

Vogt and others have studied the linguistic properties of questions to understand what makes them powerful. Questions starting with "why", "how" and "what" are most powerful (in that order), particularly if connected to an issue or activity that people feel they can genuinely engage with.

17 E. Vogt, J. Brown and D. Issacs (2003) *The art of powerful questions: catalyzing insight, innovation and action*. Whole Systems Associates. Mill Valley, CA

Take the example We saw this several years ago when a panel of experienced natural resource managers from government agencies employed us to develop a conceptual model for an important coastal lake system and its catchments, linking social and economic factors into scientific ecological models. The panel's chairman explained: "*We want the model to help us understand the cause-and-effect relationships between people and nature so we can improve our planning and decision-making processes.*"

The framework for the conceptual model was successfully developed. While it showed the task was more complex than the panel envisaged, it also revealed that people had different views on how the model might actually be used. Indeed, we sensed the model was not really the solution they needed. So we asked a question: "*How did you all decide the catchment metabolism model was the right solution?*" We asked another question: "*What were the underlying issues the model was meant to address, and why did those issues exist?*" It became apparent the panel was very concerned that unless land development and catchment management practices were changed, the health and prosperity of the region could significantly decline. Furthermore, they passionately explained their position: "*Cooperation between our organisations and with the community has to improve, otherwise we cannot expect the health of the lakes and catchments to improve.*" Emerging, future issues also needed to be identified sooner so better responses could be developed and applied than in the past. It all became clear: building a sound scientific basis for decision making was a useful activity, but the real issue was the region's capacity to imagine, motivate and manage beneficial change.

The project took a whole new direction. Developing the capacity to better understand and engage different stakeholders was now recognised by everyone as important. Their social and emotional intelligence needed to be enhanced to match and use the wealth of economic and ecological content. Panel members started reflecting on their own ways of thinking, understanding and operating. Interviews with farmers, fishermen, public servants, environmentalists and developers provided astounding insights to their concerns, relationships and aspirations for the lakes, particularly the stories they told and held to be true about how the lakes and catchments functioned and what was contributing to their decline. This culminated in the development of a guide for the natural resource management and development community to drive a dramatic improvement in the strategic thinking that underpins planning and organisational cooperation. What started out as a technical model ended up as a tool for deep reflection, holistic thinking and respectful collaboration.

Humility is an essential ingredient for the person asking the question as well as the person answering it. Our individual points of view and our ability to ask questions come from our experience and cognitive ability, shaped by our professional discipline, role, values and beliefs, and tempered by our emotional intelligence. Without humility and an open mind, these factors can combine to generate unreasonably strong views about the answers to simple and complex questions.

Questions that build understanding

Problems that matter are rarely simple. They usually involve complex webs of cause and effect that are difficult for any individual to fully appreciate. This has spawned numerous techniques to unravel the problems so we can develop more meaningful and useful solutions. Systems mapping is one technique promoted by some of the world's leading organisational strategy advisors (the Director of MIT's Sloan School of Management, Peter Senge, is probably the most well-known). Systems mapping is explored further in Chapter 7 – at its heart, the question that systems mapping aims to address is: *What are the components of the problem we are interested in and how do they relate to one another?*

Asking the question *Why does this problem exist?* will always elicit a different response from different people. This contributes different and complementary perspectives to systems mapping because values and beliefs come into play. A common tool to help build understanding is to ask "why" five times. A more rigorous approach to this task has been developed by Sohail Inyatullah, a Pakistani-born political scientist who worked in America for many years and now lives in Australia. The process Sohail has adopted is to outline the key problem and list the causes for that problem. He digs deeper to expose the world views and "stories" that influence and shape the way people think in order to make sense of situations, and how that affects their behaviour. Exposing these deep, often unconscious stories that frame our thinking allows us to talk about them, to test their robustness and usefulness, and shift them when necessary so that new choices and behaviours can emerge. Initiating change at this deeper level is ultimately more profound and enduring.

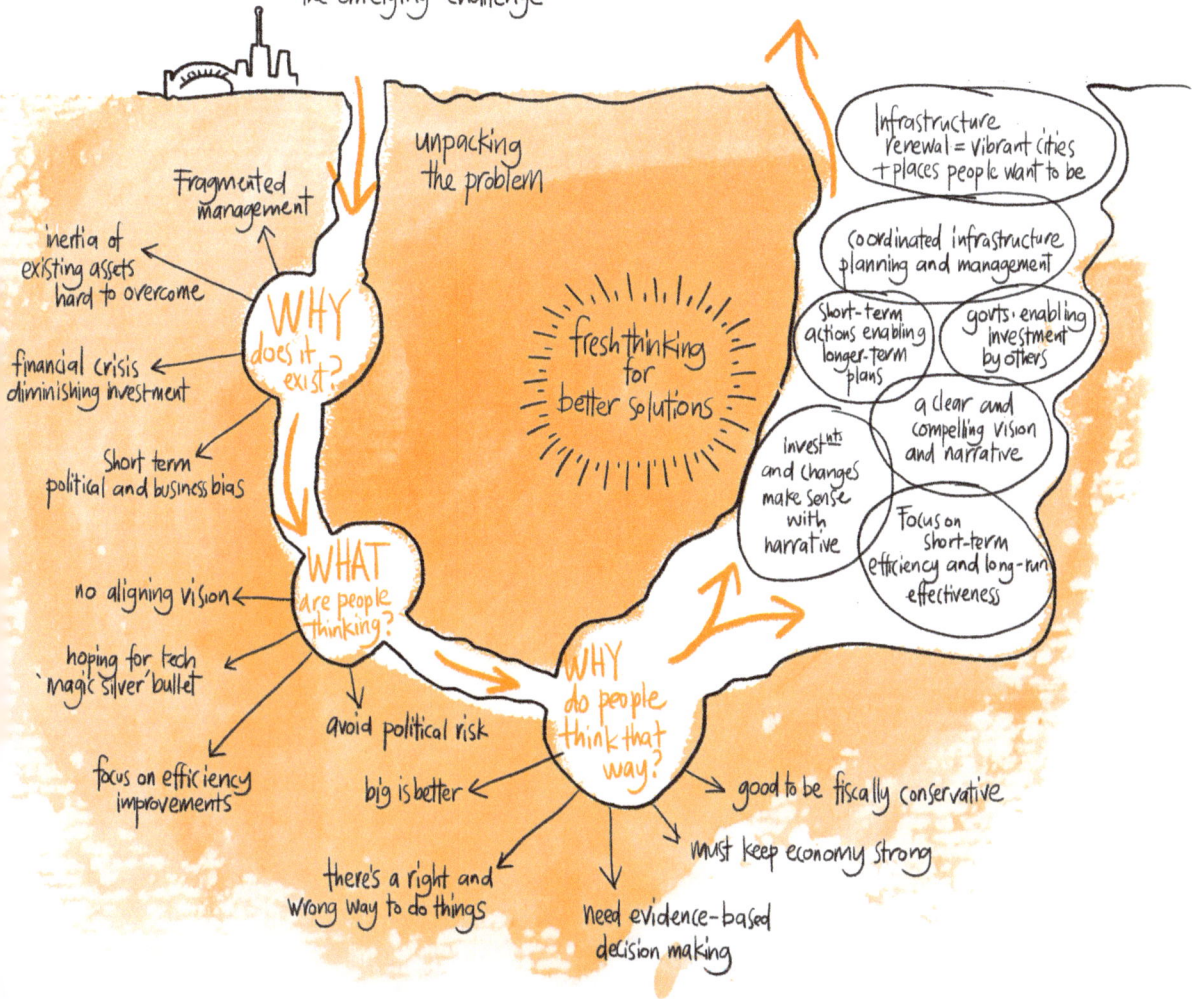

Problem:
City infrastructure is not up to the emerging challenge

unpacking the problem

Fragmented management

inertia of existing assets hard to overcome

financial crisis diminishing investment

Short term political and business bias

WHY does it exist?

WHAT are people thinking?

no aligning vision

hoping for tech 'magic silver' bullet

focus on efficiency improvements

avoid political risk

big is better

there's a right and wrong way to do things

WHY do people think that way?

good to be fiscally conservative

must keep economy strong

need evidence-based decision making

fresh thinking for better solutions

Infrastructure renewal = vibrant cities + places people want to be

Coordinated infrastructure planning and management

Short-term actions enabling longer-term plans

govts. enabling investment by others

a clear and compelling vision and narrative

investmts and changes make sense with narrative

Focus on short-term efficiency and long-run effectiveness

It's important to burrow beneath the surface of issues to understand the mindsets and stories that are at the root of our choices and behaviours. Only when we work at these deeper levels, shifting the current ways of thinking, will new solutions emerge that are likely to provide the foundation for more profound and enduring change. This figure provides a simplified view of the kinds of thinking that underpin our current infrastructure challenges, and the ways in which they could be reframed for more enduring and valuable change.

Using the power of questions 75

Problems that matter are
rarely simple.

But the simplest of questions can
build understanding and reveal
where the opportunity lies.

Simple questions, at the right time

We were once involved in discussions with a team planning an upgrade to a major highway connecting key capital cities. At a project kick-off meeting with the client and consulting team, the question we asked was: *What are the given or set parameters and conditions for this project*? Participants were then asked to jot down no more than six bullet points, individually and without discussion. Once the answers were consolidated on a whiteboard and we'd led a conversation about them, it became clear that about two-thirds of the "given conditions" for the project were actually invalid assumptions arising from previous experience; they did not apply to this particular project.

A team member summed up the feeling: *"Well, if they're not constraints, that opens a range of options to us I'd not thought possible."* Asking the question *What are the set parameters*? had expanded the creative space for the project, helping to avoid future problems, costs and time delays which the original invalid assumptions may have generated.

Questions that circumvent fear

Most of us are familiar with the idea that the greatest barrier to new thought and action is often fear – of uncertainty, failure or looking stupid. Our evolutionary survival senses are fine-tuned to perceive threats, and when combined with our Western cultural disposition to action and our reliance on people who are "right" and have the status of experts, the typical business environment can see too much risk in anything that is "less than certain". Not surprisingly, authentic conversation is unlikely to take place in a context of fear, mistrust and hierarchical control.

We've found that questions provide a powerful tonic for these situations. The question and the way it is asked can shift perceptions of risk and dilute the influence of hierarchy. For example, a challenge stated as *"I don't agree with you"* can be delivered far more constructively: *"I don't understand how that conclusion is reached. Can you help by explaining your rationale?"*

Asking open questions with a genuine intention of inquiry and learning can allow people with widely varying knowledge to legitimately contribute without fearing loss of face. Open questions are also more likely to engender sharing of knowledge and insights between people, build rapport, support sense making, and build a greater shared understanding of a situation.

Questions provided a common ground and purpose...

Take the example

The importance of asking questions was illustrated to us during a meeting we attended with a long-term CEO of a water company and his new Chair of the Board. Both were very experienced, with successful and established careers. The meeting was about the relevance of sustainability to the water company. *"Nothing has substantially changed in our industry over the past 50 years and it won't in the foreseeable future!"* was the strong-fisted opening remark from the CEO. It was a remarkable statement not just because it was a bold demonstration of authority, but because it was clearly untrue. In contrast, the new Chair of the Board was pushing for fresh thinking and believed strongly that sustainable thought and practices were critical to the future of the business. The CEO disagreed and reinforced his point: *"Our core business is pumps, pipes, and water treatment. We should not get distracted by passing fads and whims."*

It was clear that advocating a business case for sustainability at that particular moment wouldn't work. We changed tack, asking the CEO how the business had evolved and become so successful under his watch, what challenges were overcome, and why those challenges had emerged. We recorded these insights and recollections on a wall chart with a timeline so people could start to "see the bigger picture". We then explored with the Board and management team the factors that might drive change in future, and what success might look like in those conditions. It soon became clear to all that significant change in the operating environment was already well underway. Social and environmental issues were becoming more important and future success would demand greater engagement with customers. The CEO was visibly engaged in the discussion and by the challenge ahead and it was obvious he now saw our process as an opportunity to contribute his substantial knowledge to a good outcome. The discussion also saw the Chair of the Board adjust her perception of what "sustainability" meant, moving it away from low-emission vehicles and paper-saving measures to actions far more central to their customers, community and core water services. The questions we asked had provided the vehicle for reaching a common ground and purpose. A board member observed at the end of the meeting: *"Thanks a lot for this. This is the first time in 3 years of being on this Board that I feel a real purpose for the organisation and the role I can play."*

Questions that build a reason for change

The initial reaction of the water company CEO provides a great example of "conservatism masquerading as pragmatism" that we referred to in the previous chapter. To move beyond business as usual and conservative business practices, a compelling reason to change must be demonstrated.

We know most people avoid change, partly because it creates uncertainty and fear, but also because it requires effort.

The case for change must be compelling, not just at the organisational or project level but also at the personal level for those charged with leading change.

Numerous studies have shown that people are generally more motivated to avoid risk than to gain benefit (we'll run faster *from* something than *toward* something).

The distinguished American neuroeconomist, neuroscientist, doctor and writer, Dr Gregory Berns, provides an interesting and relevant insight.[18] His research has found the brains of people aged below 30 years are more plastic and able to rewire, which generally makes them open to new ideas and adaptation. Risk and novelty can be attractive to this age group. Older people are conversely less able and open, so familiarity and closeness to existing experiences and things are more important. Thus what triggers engagement within a group, and a reason to change, are likely to depend at least in part on age. This is one of the many factors we take into account when developing and presenting questions to challenge the status quo and generate ongoing benefits.

It's vital that questions relate to things within the bounds of possibility for people to influence. Otherwise the questions are seen as "academic curiosities", not questions that warrant attention and thought. Common questions we ask project teams are quite simple:

1 What are the major risks to this project during its design and construction phase?

2 What new or different risks are likely to exist over its operating life?

3 What business initiatives are your peers undertaking that we can learn from?

4 Is the project developing in a way that's consistent with core business strategy?

5 Will the project be well regarded in 5 or 10 years' time?

---

18 Particularly worth reading is Berns' book, *Iconoclast: A Neuroscientist Reveals How to Think Differently* (Harvard Business Review Press, 2010). In this book, Berns argues that no organisation can survive without iconoclasts – innovators who single-handedly upturn conventional wisdom and manage to achieve what so many others deem impossible.

Generating insight through diversity

Apart from his interest in how our brains change as we age, Dr Berns also likes to explore how great innovators see things differently. His research concludes it's primarily because they don't fall into the mental efficiency traps that others do. They remain aware and vigilant against the over-use of mental categorisations, which he describes as "death to imagination".

So where do new ideas come from, and when are we most likely to have them? The answer is that answers mostly come from unfamiliar situations. When we're in familiar situations we tend to think in familiar ways. Our brains are quite literally "wired by our experiences". To ensure we respond quickly and efficiently, our brains create "mental maps" to help us interpret situations quickly without much conscious thought. Repetition through behaviour or deliberately practising reinforces the neural pathways that make these mental maps. While this makes thought and routine tasks efficient, it has a downside – we perceive only the sensations we are programmed to receive. Our awareness is further restricted by the fact that we recognise only solutions we have mental maps for – we see what we expect to see.

This is where new situations, new people and new questions come into play, challenging the brain to discard its usual categories of perception and create new ones. Novelty unshackles the brain from past experiences and forces it to make new judgements. Perception can be changed through experience.

As drivers of sustainable development, we need to help people "reframe" to find better solutions, employing different analytical methods, exposing them to people with different and complementary knowledge and experience, and asking questions that challenge them to interpret situations from a different perspective.

One single question can change the complete project

Take the example One of our great satisfactions is watching project teams shift their perceptions to surprise themselves with the innovative solutions they can develop. One team we worked with was designing and delivering a power station and high-voltage transmission line for a new mine in south-east Asia. The project manager advised us the project was relatively routine, well defined and a small component of the overall mine development. "*I'm not sure talking further about the core scope and design solution is really warranted,*" he said. "*After all, it's a routine project. We could deliver this in our sleep.*" Despite misgivings, he conceded to a team workshop to see if any good ideas to improve the project emerged.

Reluctantly, the project team also accepted the involvement of Angus, a colleague in their business they had little to do with. Angus had a background in international development and it was clear the team doubted he could add much value to their project. We began the workshop by talking about the power station and transmission line, and importantly, its local context. "*Do you want to know about the local militia groups?*" asked Angus. Stunned silence. What did militia groups have to do with this project? Angus explained that the local people had long been frustrated by the lack of energy to support agricultural and urban development. Militia groups tapped into this dissatisfaction to gain support – and they often blew up privately owned power facilities.

The project team reflected on the 65 km of power line they planned to string across the landscape. With that single item of information the team recognised the design requirements and scope of their project had completely changed – so too had their perceptions of the project, the workshop and the value of including a colleague from another field of practice.

Narrowing focus increases risk

It is often tempting and politically safe to engage technical experts to provide answers to complicated problems, but this can carry real risks. By definition, experts have deep specialist expertise in a topic or field of endeavour; they are not generalists. This carries with it an interesting and important neurological connection. We learn and retain knowledge by creating and reinforcing the physical neural pathways in our brain. Experts have highly honed neural pathways that reinforce certain ways of understanding; they conceptually and physiologically see the world a certain way. Experts have made great investments in establishing their knowledge base and neurological connections, which thus present substantial barriers to wanting to or being able to change them. The experts and the people who engage them can assume the expert understands the full nature of the problem and has the "right" answer. Almost by definition this is not the case.

So while it can be valuable to engage experts in solving complicated problems, it is likely to be valuable, almost necessary, to engage people with relevant but different experience and discipline backgrounds to get a richer, more realistic picture of the problem, and thus generate viable solutions.

The global financial crisis has provided numerous examples of how "things can go wrong" when particular ideologies and perspectives dominate. Alan Greenspan was lauded as one of the most successful leaders of the US Federal Reserve when he retired in 2006 after 16 years managing the world's biggest economy. Just 2 years later he was facing hard questions at the government's inquiry into the causes of the financial crisis. In his testimony to the 2008 House Committee on Oversight and Government Reform, Greenspan attempted to explain how he and other experts failed to see the risks in financial markets. Greenspan conceded he had "found a flaw" in his model – he and his peers had presumed that the self-interest of lending institutions would protect shareholder equity. This had influenced everyone's approach to risk management:

"The whole intellectual edifice…collapsed…because the data input to the risk management models generally covered only the past two decades, a period of euphoria. Had instead the models been fitted more appropriately to historical periods of stress, capital requirements would have been much higher and the financial world would be in far better shape today in my judgment."[19]

Greenspan and his colleagues made a mistake more common than most people appreciate – they assumed their perspective would always be correct and would always achieve the best results – but on this occasion of course, the results were catastrophic.

19 http://democrats.oversight.house.gov/images/stories/documents/20081023100438.pdf

Questioning to drive new solutions

Entirely new ideas and solutions can emerge remarkably quickly in response to carefully crafted questions that challenge business-as-usual. Consider the challenges associated with the development of coal seam and shale gas fields around the world. Concerns over land access, water management and pollution have caused significant opposition to the industry, eroding its social licence to operate, causing delays and increasing development costs. What approach might the industry take if it asked the question: *How can we develop and operate gas fields so that communities welcome them?*

A potential response to the question above could be: *Extract the gas in situ rather than extracting much of the water above it to liberate the gas,* to which a "developing question" would be: *How can we get access to information on technology that will enable in-situ gas extraction, recognising it might exist in a range of industries?* Another response could have been: *Engage the community and land-holders as shareholders in the gas field development,* to which a developing question might be: *How could we establish an equitable, affordable and transparent scheme of dividends that the community will endorse?*

Further development of ideas into viable solutions is possible by using questions with parameters to evaluate and filter the ideas. The point is: questioners should allow and encourage ideas to develop, preventing premature judgement and using questions to push through problems by continually fostering a mindset of inquiry and problem solving.

why?

how? what?

where? which?
when? who?

yes/no

Providing certainty with a clear process

The tendency of Western cultures to recognise and reward people for quick responses and action is reflected in many of the infrastructure sectors we work across. These sectors tend toward the conservative, partly because the things they provide (such as a water and energy supplies) are considered essential services that require high reliability – so they avoid change that might threaten this. When planners, engineers, investors and other experts apply suites of technical and investment standards, innovation *can* be difficult to motivate let alone deliver. How do we engender practical new ideas and translate them into on-ground action?

We find it's essential to clearly articulate the "design development" process because, if done thoughtfully, it reduces the anxiety and risk perceived by people participating in that process who will otherwise thwart engagement and imagination. *Is this a good use of my time, will it produce any ideas we haven't already thought of, and will anyone really do anything with the ideas that do get produced*? Enhancing certainty reduces the stress people feel, freeing them to contribute more constructively. It can also help suspend judgement and the desire to "jump straight to a solution, any solution" and promotes the ambiguity of early problem-solving phases not as a risk but as an opportunity to collect information and build knowledge.

Innovating – with a little help

The practice of creating and using powerful questions benefits from a good coach. One of the world's most well-known business coaches is Rosamund Zander, a pioneering American psychotherapist in the field of leadership and relationships. Her husband is the renowned British-born musician and orchestra conductor, Benjamin Zander, who also coaches youth orchestras. In their best-selling book *The Art of Possibility*,[20] they promote the idea that creativity is an innate adult capacity – we can all do it if shown how. They describe their professional teaching roles as a process that helps students "chip away at the barriers" that block their abilities and expression.

We see a parallel with our role as design coaches on projects or sustainability leaders in organisations – we coach professional teams to help them chip away the barriers to develop smarter and more sustainable solutions. The challenge we enjoy is answering the question: *What are the powerful questions that will provide most benefit to this team*?

Sure, not everyone is naturally innovative, but everyone can improve their ideas and their application. It just takes practice. It's like learning to ride a bike – the first time is hard, the second a little easier, and after a while it's effortless and requires little conscious thought.

We've found it helps to make the experience enjoyable and interesting, matching the mood with the task; upbeat music can set a tone and energetic facilitation can also help. Then when the ideas start to flow, the "aha!" moments of insight and discovery ignite the pleasure centres in the participants' brains. This enhances their feeling of satisfaction and perceived status – and thus the desire to repeat the activity. Innovation can become easier and more appealing.

Without questions, we get nowhere. Indeed, questions are one of the most powerful items in our tool bag.

Questions have driven development of human thought and action throughout time. Powerful questions reveal new insights and ideas, enabling new and better solutions. So spend time working out what questions really matter. Sometimes these questions can take us in unexpected directions, which can seem to increase complexity. But don't worry; methods exist to navigate complexity to find more effective, elegant solutions. The next chapter focuses on the fundamental step that's required.

20   Rosamund and Benjamin Zander (2000) *The Art of Possibility*, Penguin Group, New York

USESFUL QUESTIONS

- **How do we know we've identified the questions that really matter?**

- **What are the questions that will provide most benefit to this team or situation?**

- **What assumptions are we making, and are they valid?**

Seven

Taking a step back

Everything sits within a wider context.

Systems thinking is critical to fully understanding the problem.

Taking a step back helps find breakthrough solutions.

"If I had an hour to solve a problem
I'd spend 55 minutes thinking
about the problem and 5 minutes
thinking about solutions."

Albert Einstein

Things are defined in relation to other things – what's real, what are risks, and what interventions are possible. So looking at the bigger picture is never a waste of time. It's the first step in thinking more systemically about the nature and scope of the real problem.

Take the example of electricity substations in a capital city. They are essential infrastructure for a reliable power supply, but they increasingly bear the brunt of community opposition, with development applications of many substations in urban areas being more frequently refused by local councils. The design manager decided it was time to "take a step back" from detailed design and explore how they could approach this differently. "*After all*", he said, "*we have been designing these for years and maybe we could refresh our approach.*" But he was also somewhat sceptical that strategic thinking about more sustainable infrastructure would make any material difference.

So when some surprising findings emerged after we mapped out the way the context had changed for substations over previous and future decades, he became very engaged. In short, it showed that almost all the key factors had changed. Community expectations about visual amenity and safety had increased over the years and more extreme temperatures could now affect sensitive instruments. There were new and imminent regulations aimed at reducing greenhouse gas emissions and reducing flood risk and damage, and greater demand for more sophisticated skills to manage the complex operating systems of today's substations.

But it wasn't until a team member asked "*So how are we thinking about the changing transmission network architecture*"? that the discussion really got interesting. The likelihood of more local power generation through small-scale solar or co-generation systems would change the function and capacity of the substation into the future. New sources of power from solar, wind farms or biogas plants would supplement the previous supply sourced from a single, centralised power station.

The future was shaping up very differently, with many micro-scale, distributed sources of power, a decentralised transmission network, rising community expectations as to what was acceptable, and an environment subject to greater weather extremes. It changed many of the set notions about the "best" design. It also triggered other opportunities from the design manager: "*We really need to look at an earlier and better process to select the sites for these substations. Often they had been chosen many years ago, but are now surrounded by suburban development and sensitive land uses that cause real problems.*"

Why take a step back?

We enjoy, and understandably value and reward, problem-solving and solution-finding. Every project is a response to a problem or need that has to be resolved. This, plus a budget to spend, a tight deadline and expectations of delivery means there is a driving momentum to "get on with it" – to start work, get straight into detail, decide the solutions and start producing. That's fine – but the first step we should take is actually a step back from the detail and solution. Why? To explore all the opportunities and to ask: *What's possible*?

Taking the time at the start of a project to better understand its wider and connected context is critical because no project or organisation operates in isolation.

Expanding the sense of a project's boundaries and identifying key linkages will always shift thinking and challenge assumptions – and from our experience, it delivers better solutions. Taking a narrow view of any project's context will only ever see narrowly defined approaches and solutions. It's also worth noting that increasingly, we see the likely "derailers" of projects sitting well outside the immediate project boundary. These derailers are often not even recognised as a risk until things go wrong.

Take the example Sometimes extending the thinking of a team changes the project's objective, as we experienced on a high-volume minerals port in the Asia-Pacific. As the region's mineral potential was realised, the port was struggling to meet demand and a US$2 billion upgrade was announced. Initial assumptions were that constructing an additional berth and more unloading and storage facilities would solve the issue. The team had been focussed on the detailed design options until we mapped the whole system round the port – from the mine and rail connections to the port and shipping traffic. This initiated a complete re-think of the project. Looking beyond the port site, the team identified that the rail system which transported the minerals to the port for export was also at capacity and unable to serve an expanded port. In addition, while the port was struggling to meet demand it was acknowledged there was substantial scope to improve its productivity – by far the better business strategy. Expanding the port's facilities would do little to lift its productivity and this solution began increasingly to look like a risk.

A different solution emerged for the project team. Improving the capacity and logistics of the rail system (and not the port) would increase the volume of minerals to the port. Reducing the need or at least the scale of the upgrade would make it less complex and substantially less expensive to operate. Taking this approach also triggered discussions about the underlying causes of the port's low productivity and ways to improve it. By looking outside the site boundary and mapping the inter-connected operating environment of the port, the team had a different understanding of the real problem. This changed their thinking about the best solutions, and what was possible to achieve with an ultimately more sustainable and viable outcome.

As one participant reflected: *"We initially looked at this only from a port design perspective. But talking to the rail and freight logistics people shed a different light on the problem, and opened up new solutions."* This allowed the project to proceed in an integrated way from the outset, rather than designing solutions first, and considering how to manage the impacts later.

The value of systems

Taking a step back allows us to think systemically, to understand the whole context with all its inter-relationships and linkages. These connections are vital in identifying the root causes of problems and all the flow-on effects. Systems thinking is challenging for many people we work with – their professional training encourages a very structured approach that follows a linear flow of logic. If you ask a team to develop a schematic "map" of their project as a system, a common response will be to start with a bullet-pointed list of issues.

Mapping the project as a system – a network that has linkages and flows from the site to local, regional and national scales – presents a powerful visual picture of a connected context.

What does this look like in practice? When we asked a project team to draw their project (a power plant upgraded to be fuelled with gas), this is what they drew:

gas pipeline   gas treatment   power station   transmission

We then worked with the team to develop a systems map of the same project, which considered all the elements, connections and flows at various scales. Their second attempt at drawing the project is below. You can see it's markedly different, giving a much richer picture and a more accurate reflection of the actual context, with all its elements and flows.

It's surprising how systems mapping brings clarity to the highest-priority challenges, and where they occur across the whole system. It also engenders a very different sense of not just where important issues manifest across the project and system, but how integrated solutions could develop.

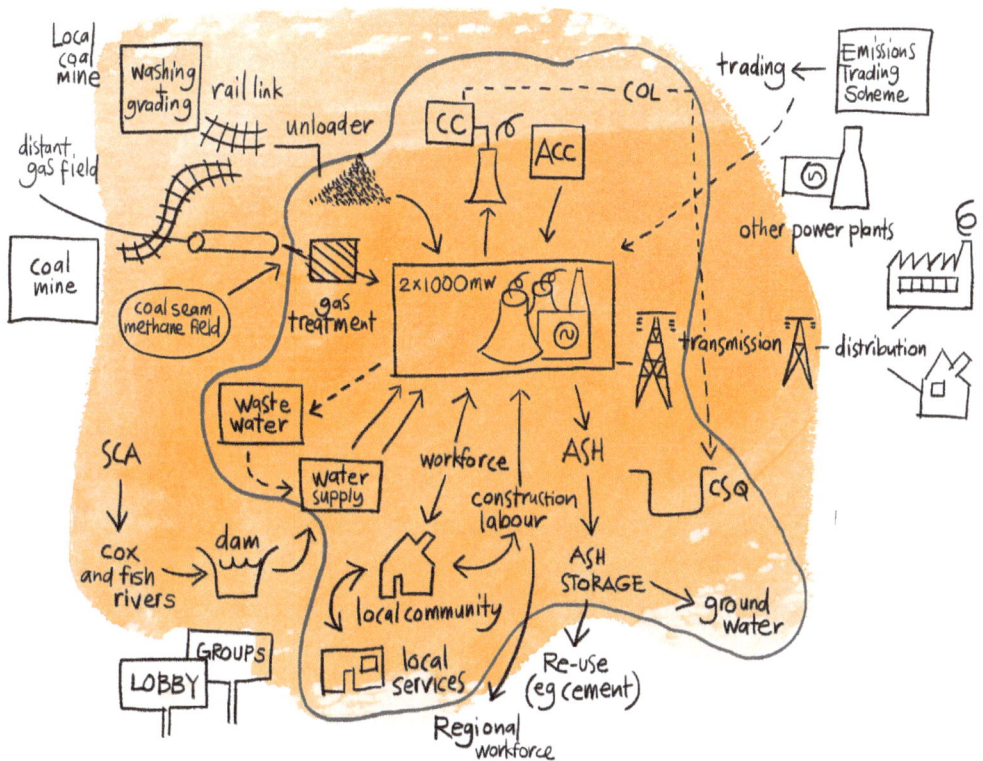

Fit for the future

Most projects we work on have a long operating life spanning decades. Many have the potential to shape communities, cities or even nations well into the future. Thinking forward helps ensure the long-term relevance and efficiency of these projects. We refer to this as "anticipatory design" or "future proofing" – because it responds to the dynamic context as well as macro trends. Designing assets that are "fit for the future" and do not just meet immediate needs is important for infrastructure that is adaptable and remains relevant to future requirements. It encourages us to understand a project's future operating environment and the implications for design decisions now. Retrofitting is always costly as it usually involves disruption in operations and supply, and redesign of linked pieces of infrastructure along with their relocation on the site.

What's required to take a step back?

It's important to keep in mind that this need not be a complex, lengthy or expensive process, but it does need a logical and a well-structured process. Useful tools to foster strategic thinking are important, as is effective facilitation to get the most from the investment in the team, whether it has a few members or many. A few important steps are:

- **Project system** – Map the physical elements or components of the project and the linkages or flows between them as part of a connected web or network. Work across a range of spatial scales, from local to regional and beyond. Think about where the project boundary might lie.

- **Issues and risks** – Assess critical risks and challenges across multiple perspectives, including technological change now and at key stages in the future. How do they change across the project life? Understand any connections between issues, and identify the issues of highest priority. What are the economic, legal and social expressions of the most challenging issues?   What are their root causes, not just their superficial manifestations?

- **Stakeholders** – Who is a stakeholder – at various scales (local, regional, national and beyond)? Who are the *priority* stakeholders with the greatest interest and influence over the project's success?   How might they change across the project phases?

- **The design challenge** – Identify the top two or three design challenges. Apply your insights about the project as a system, the rich picture of risks and issues, the way stakeholders link to these, and how you might design the problem out, and design in the benefit and long-term value. Challenge yourself. Can you make the problem an asset?

Issues wheel

Issues wheel

ENVIRONMENTAL

ECONOMIC

TECHNOLOGICAL

LEGAL

POLITICAL

SOCIAL

30 years

3 years

final land use

Legacy left in region after project

withdrawal of water

changing land use

City acceptance

LAND ACCESS

• FIFO workforce in local community

influenced by social response

rehabilitation of field
• impact on groundwater
• waste disposal
• water disposal

construction impacts— noise/waste traffic etc.

2 speed economy
tensions due to short term returns from gas vs long term returns from Ag

⇑ rents
⇑ costs
schools
children

• Govt. need for royalties
• capacity of local govt.

energy intensive infra (desal. pumps)

• change in legislation (more restrictive)

• evap. ponds— ground sterilisation
• reinjection
• fracing

• continuity of supply (contract conditions)

Production capacity

Rather than creating lists of disconnected issues, project risks and challenges can be rapidly mapped onto an Issues Wheel. Then connections between risks can be explored across various time dimensions. This helps bring clarity to the real risks and priorities, and provides a basis for a more integrated and effective response.

An important benefit of systems mapping is its visual dimension, replacing what is often "the conceptual and complex" with a grounded and "real" picture of a project's context across the local, regional and national scale. A typical comment we hear on project teams when systems mapping is: *"The team knows all about the project – we're well across it."* Yet as we get into the activity, the comments change: *"I didn't know the road was part of the project!"* or *"I hadn't considered how the rail system connected to the local towns"*, or *"I thought water was just a site management issue – but now I see the wider connections well beyond the site."* Individual team members have a store of knowledge and different understandings which, when shared collectively, can uncover new possibilities and opportunities.

Stepping back for innovation

We encourage this thinking because it provides a rich source of insights that can deliver more innovative responses to the complex challenges that projects face. Organisations almost universally value innovation, but often under-invest in the process needed to create it. Diving into the detail reinforces a "doing what we've always done" approach, and while you'll usually gain incremental improvements, rarely will you produce substantive innovation that addresses the most complex and serious risks.

Take time to imagine what's possible.

Importantly, the systems mapping discussed earlier provides a powerful basis for understanding the causality of problems and thus where more effective interventions can occur. Issues can even be eliminated altogether. More innovative and value-creating solutions are typically the result.

Typically, people start work on a project developing and evaluating options for the expected or "business as usual" solution. Time hasn't been taken for imagination and exploring what's possible. Nor is it likely that the real complexity of today's typical projects will have been unpacked and understood. The scope for innovation will therefore have been substantially reduced. So we should take a step back and take at least a little time for divergent thinking before converging on preferred options and detailed designs.

(Used with permission; Jason Clark, *Minds at Work* 2009)

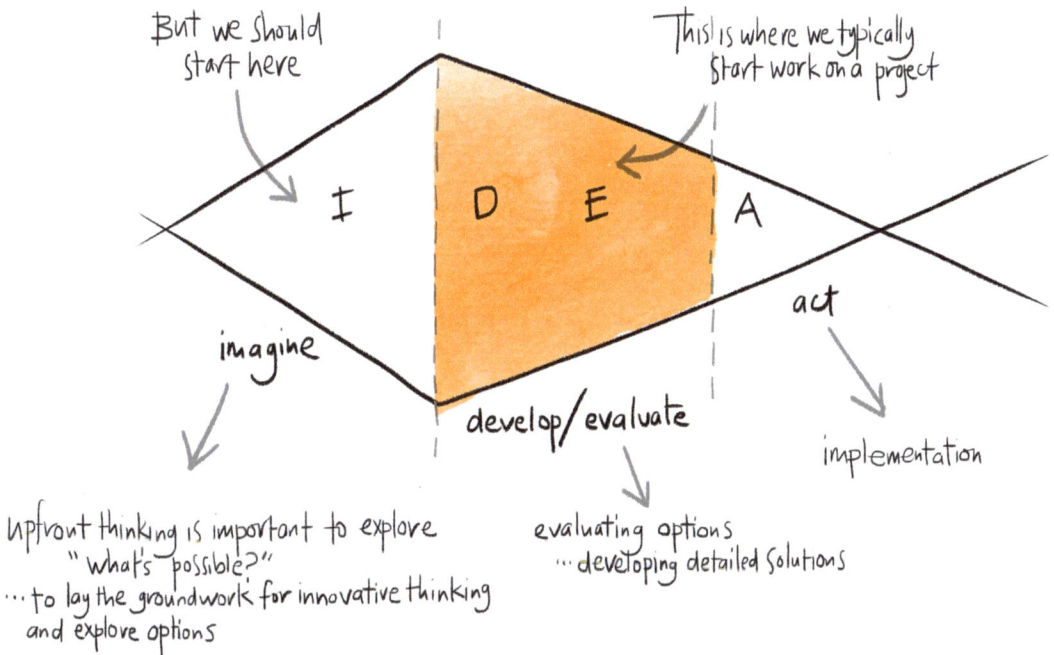

But we should start here

This is where we typically start work on a project

I   D   E   A

imagine

develop/evaluate

act

implementation

upfront thinking is important to explore
    "what's possible?"
...to lay the groundwork for innovative thinking
    and explore options

evaluating options
    ...developing detailed solutions

The value of diversity

Working with team members who possess similar skill-sets to our own is the norm, which readily creates silos of people with the same perspectives. Seeing the problem in its wider context and with different expertise offering different perspectives is part of stepping back.

The more astute business leaders are recognising the worth of this process. Having the "right" mix of expertise is important. From our experience, there is always value in involving different expertise in strategic thinking sessions. Different experts ask different sets of questions, view the problem differently, and add a new perspective.

(Take the example) The benefits of different disciplines played out on a team planning a major mining project in an African country. They had asked us to help identify sustainable approaches to major challenges. A waste expert was invited along, but no one expected him to play a serious role in the discussion. Things quickly changed when discussions turned to the energy source for a planned new port and associated infrastructure as part of the mining project. The initial approach was to construct a power plant that required imported gas or fossil fuels to produce energy – but the waste expert saw other opportunities. These included using a proven and cost-effective technology to convert waste from a nearby city into a biomass energy source for the power plant. This would reduce the plant's environmental impacts, generate local opportunities, assist the city with its waste management, use what was a waste product as a resource, and help the mining company build a social licence. Without the waste expert, it's doubtful these results would have been realised. His reflections are interesting. *"I started out the day wondering how on earth I could contribute to this – I was quite sceptical. But I was soon engrossed in the process that gradually took us to different thinking. We ended up with solutions that would not have been possible without it."*

UNDERSTANDING THE CONNECTIONS

Systems mapping will highlight the complexity of the context for infrastructure projects today, and will also uncover the implications and risk of issues such as changing community expectations and legislative regimes across the whole life of the project. Pigeon-holing them as "environmental" or "community" issues also creates risk and inadequate responses, because most issues are not one-dimensional, but are expressed across multiple dimensions. Environmental issues usually have a strong social expression, and also legal, political and economic implications.

Take the example The inter-connectedness of project issues was evident from our experience helping to plan a major coastal power plant in Asia that was needed to meet the power needs of a mining project some distance inland. By mapping the project's broader context and key challenges, the project team identified 17 major issues that would affect its success. Of these, not one was *solely* an environmental, social or economic issue – each issue had significant implications across all three dimensions.

Two examples illustrate this. The discharge of water from the plant into the bay had the potential to degrade corals and fishing grounds. This was initially seen as an environmental issue to be managed by marine scientists. But understanding all the stakeholders and the flow-on effects quickly identified this as being important to local villagers and their livelihoods – and their concerns might ultimately be supported and acted on by politicians. The quality of water discharges was also linked to many other aspects of the infrastructure design, and all needed consideration when thinking about the total impact. The discharge would have caused opposition to the project, and raise political, investor and reputation concerns. It was not just an environmental issue. The community engagement and social impact teams quickly became involved with marine scientists and design engineers. A better understanding of the total impact led to re-thinking water discharges along with the whole use of water in the plant.

Furthermore, while the design for discharge of cooling water into the bay met current international performance standards, it was sailing close to the acceptable water quality and temperature limits, with little buffer. All the indications pointed to more stringent standards being implemented in the foreseeable future. Costly redesign and disruption to the plant was therefore likely. Looking at this broader context over time identified this risk for the project and reinforced the merit of designing with the future in mind.

The provision of an electricity supply to the project is another example. The initial solution was to build a power plant on the site to generate power just for the project. But the community and political expectations were quite different. Many had suffered unreliable electricity supplies for years, and saw an opportunity they had been waiting for to gain a reliable power supply for general community benefit. This triggered a re-think of the purpose of the project's energy generation. What was initially seen as a task for the power engineers quickly became one for the whole project team.

Silos equal risk

Elements of projects that flow across multiple tasks and disciplines can be poorly recognised or underplayed. Even if they are recognised, the response is usually conceived through a single perspective, or focuses on operational and short-term responses. An approach that analyses the project's part in the wider system over the whole project life will spotlight those elements that can otherwise easily slide beneath the radar. It will also assess them through a different and fresh lens to generate different ideas, options and solutions.

Our work with a global resources company to develop and implement a waste strategy across the business highlights this. The initial strategy was set by the strategy section of the business, but they had no ability to influence implementation at the operational level. The operational staff responsible for implementing the strategy had no insight as to why the strategy had certain objectives, and what they needed to do differently to deliver on these. They had no ownership and limited understanding of its drivers and rationale.

Our approach was to take a step back and design a process that involved the strategy team as well as the operational staff.

We mapped the waste process across the company and its stakeholders and suppliers as a total system and looked at all the challenges and emerging drivers. This was the first time the operators fully understood the complexities, the inter-relationships and the need to change previous practice. They acknowledged that the data they had been collecting for years was no longer informative to respond to the changing imperatives relating to waste. Information on total tonnage of waste collected was not sufficient; what was needed for good waste management was reliable data on waste composition, recycling, re-use and waste avoidance options. This changed their motivations, priorities and, importantly, their actions.

Mapping the integrated systems of waste was the turning point, as it highlighted the interrelated nature of today's operating environment for many projects and organisations.

Being able to systematically diagnose the causes of the problem is a crucial first step. Then thinking and acting collaboratively is what enables solutions to take maximum effect, and this is our focus in the next chapter.

USEFUL QUESTIONS

- **Where would you draw the boundary of your project?**

- **What were the two most challenging issues on a recent project that were located outside the project site boundary?**

- **What changes are likely in locations upstream and downstream of the site that could seriously impact on the project into the future?**

- **How well does your team understand all the connections and inter-relationships of their project across various scales?**

Eight

Consciously collaborate

Insight, inspiration and ideas collide through collaboration.

Trust and transparency are essential ingredients for successful collaboration.

Collaboration aligns effort, helps manage risk and allows us to do more with less.

"In the long history of humankind ... those who learned to collaborate and improvise most effectively have prevailed."

Charles Darwin, naturalist

"Collaboration continues to be viewed as one of the few models that can catalyse solutions to the sustainable development challenges we face at the speed and scale that we need." This was a key conclusion expressed in 2012 by 800 experts across 74 countries representing business, government, non-government and academic perspectives.[21]

Indeed it's not hard to find endorsement of multi-stakeholder collaboration as a key tool in achieving genuine societal progress and business success. Pick up virtually any report addressing contemporary challenges around cities, infrastructure, productivity and the like, and you'll find recommendations for greater collaboration between key stakeholders.

In 2006, The Economist Intelligence Unit interviewed several hundred executives worldwide and concluded "the future belongs to those who collaborate". Executives felt their markets were becoming ever more global, with the ripple effect including functions in their organisation atomising across more geographies and partners, and competition from all regions of the world intensifying.[22] Sound familiar? They advised that to succeed in such an environment, organisations would need to collaborate with specialist players from customers to partners to competitors and research organisations. It was noted that while firms have traditionally collaborated vertically – with suppliers and distributors – the need for agility in a fast-changing environment will drive companies to increase collaboration of all types so they can move quickly, work efficiently and effectively and continue to prosper.

We agree, for two primary reasons. Firstly, the drivers of change anticipated above are already apparent and impacting businesses. Secondly, and more importantly, our experience tells us transformative business and project solutions can be achieved (sometimes necessarily) via collaboration.

But what do we mean by "collaboration"?

21 Globescan, SustainAbility (2012) *Collaborating for a sustainable future*, Survey.
    http://www.sustainability.com/library/collaborating-for-a-sustainable-future
22 The Economist (2007) *Collaboration – transforming the way business works*,
    A report from the Economist Intelligence Unit (sponsored by Cisco Systems), New York

More than the sum of the parts

Many executives would argue that their organisations are already actively collaborating with customers, suppliers and interest groups. This is true, and consistent with a pure definition of collaboration: "working together" or "willingly cooperating". Yet while this collaboration may be incurring a higher level of business-to-business interaction and stakeholder communication than has typically occurred in the past, we believe it often falls well short of the contemporary intent. People are still largely playing well-defined, conventional and transactional business and professional roles to get the job done.

Today, collaboration means more than just labouring side by side; it's bringing people together from different backgrounds to foster a collision of insights and inspire better ideas, and partnering to apply each other's strengths to achieve substantially more than either party could achieve alone.

Innovative partnerships can be found in the fields of pharmaceutical research and consumer- driven product development and marketing. Some of the best examples of collaboration occur in the open-source programming community, where people voluntarily contribute in proportion to their "comparative advantage" – that is, their passion, skills, talent and efficiency.

Such innovative partnerships are less common in the sectors delivering, owning and operating private or public infrastructure. Outcome-driven alliancing is one of the models of project delivery that is most suited to, and likely to support, the sort of creative collaboration we are advocating. Yet irrespective of the business model, these sectors can be more conservative, adversarial and slow to change, meaning that creative business practices can be slow to take root. But the pressure for change is on, given the vast sums of money involved, the demand for new and better infrastructure, and the lower rates of productivity that have emerged in some sectors in recent years.

In 2011, the British Cabinet Minister Francis Maude picked up on this theme in describing his government's Big Society Initiative to distribute decision-making power and opportunity away from central government: *"I want to see a whole mix of providers. New models like public sector staff forming co-ops to run their services and civil society organisations forming new alliances with government and the private sector can drive this change. They will break down the old fashioned public service hierarchies."*[23]

So the question can no longer be *which* organisation should deliver a service or project, but how organisations across sectors can organise to produce the best outcome.

23   Deloitte (2011) XBC: *creating public value by unleashing the power of cross-boundary collaboration*, Deloitte Development LLC, New York

partnerships for a better Solution.

Take the example A private equity investor had made a major investment in developing social infrastructure, building 50 new aged-care facilities in the United Kingdom over 10 years. The technical issues in constructing the facilities were not really a problem. The major challenge was identifying suitable sites and traversing the planning approvals and community engagement processes in a timely way. It almost seemed impossible.

Did a workable solution exist?

With a little reframing of the challenge, the potential of collaboration was quickly spotted. Instead of conducting a bottom-up search for sites and following the standard planning processes, expressions of interest could be sought from cities and counties where these facilities were required. Furthermore, if thoughtfully designed, some of the new features of the aged care facilities, such as swimming pools, catering and laundry facilities, could be shared with the wider community. In this way, there was the potential to attract a level of co-investment from the local shires as well as a shared interest and support to gain planning approvals, which could enhance the overall pace and success of the venture.

The benefits of collaboration

So why is there such strong advocacy for collaboration, particularly when one might expect a depressed global economic environment to drive greater competition?

In theory there are multiple reasons.

Aligning effort – From a sustainable development perspective, it is widely recognised that many of the issues faced by society are bigger and more complex than any single discipline or organisation can resolve. Solutions require simultaneous changes in regulations, taxes and pricing, technology, business-to-business relationships and so on, thus requiring the involvement and alignment of multiple entities possessing the right mix of skills and influence. It requires strength in numbers around a common purpose.

Influencing with credibility – Every organisation has a defined purpose and set of objectives. For commercial enterprises, it is often delivery of a good or service through which profit is derived, providing a return on investment for its shareholders. Irrespective of organisation type, the singularity of purpose can make it difficult to lead thinking and advocate positions (such as on public policy matters or the merits of a major development project). By contrast, groups composed of collaborating organisations can carry greater credibility and influence because they are not perceived as advocating for narrow sectional interests.

The Aldersgate Group in the United Kingdom provides a first-class example of the energy and value that genuine collaboration generates for participants. The Group is an alliance of leaders from business, politics and society that drives action to accelerate the transition to a low-carbon, resource-efficient and competitive economy. It punches well above its weight in influencing public policy for two primary reasons:

a) its cross-industry membership enables access to their knowledge bases and connections to gain an early insight into the policy formation process, and

b) the Group engages with key decision makers in a proactive, constructive and impartial way, importantly bringing a considered and agreed multi-industry view.

Sitting government ministers subsequently endorsed the contribution of the Aldersgate Group,[24] saying it was "genuinely progressive and path breaking" and "helped inform, nourish, sustain and drive forward the progressive thinking that ultimately has informed our policies."

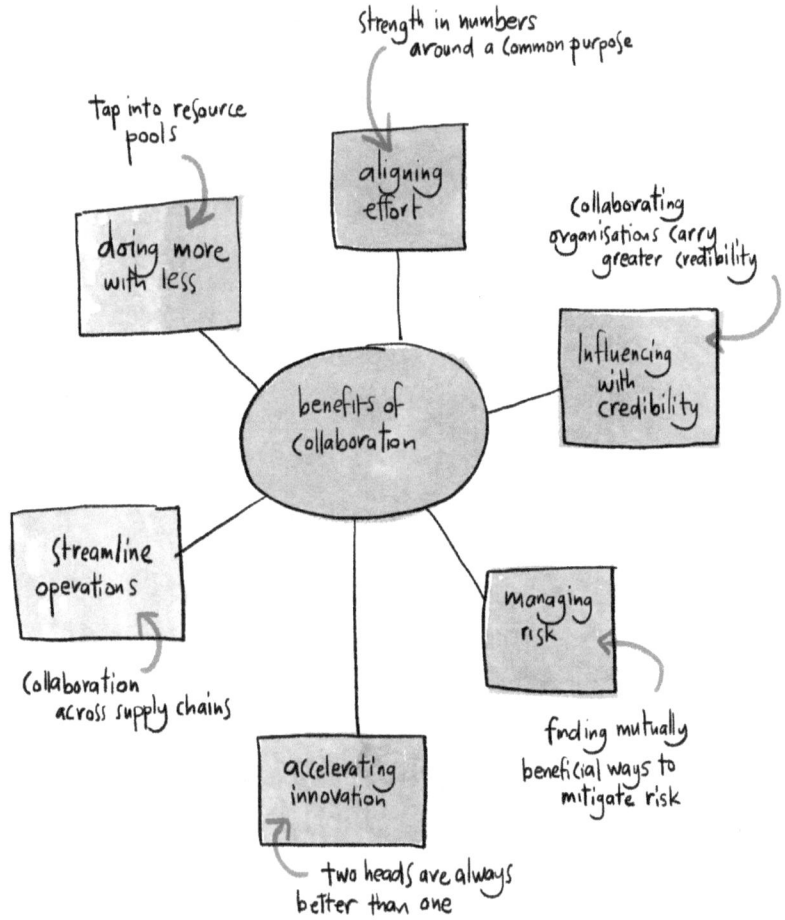

24 http://www. aldersgategroup.org.uk/ about/endorsements

Strength in numbers around a common purpose

Tap into resource pools

aligning effort

doing more with less

Collaborating organisations carry greater credibility

Influencing with credibility

benefits of collaboration

Streamline operations

managing risk

Collaboration across supply chains

accelerating innovation

finding mutually beneficial ways to mitigate risk

two heads are always better than one

Managing risk – Challenges faced by organisations can be outside their control to remedy. By involving other stakeholders or organisations in initiatives where there is shared interest, it's often possible to find mutually beneficial ways to mitigate these risks.

Accelerating innovation – The idea that good ideas can only come from within is passé. We find that people from different disciplines, organisations or interest groups bring complementary experience, insights and ideas that can enrich understanding and improve the potential for innovative solutions. So where traditional methods are unlikely to be useful or successful and there is a need for a new or better solutions, the old maxim "two heads are better than one" applies.

Streamlining operations – What represents a risk for one organisation, or potentially an inefficient use of organisational resources, can provide an opportunity for another, so collaboration along and across supply chains can help remove constraints and develop more profitable business arrangements. This is particularly relevant as organisations move to shed risk and cost by specialising in areas that are most tightly aligned with their core business and distinguishing capabilities.

Doing more with less – These collaborations need not be expensive, indeed they often tap into vast and inexpensive resource pools that may not be motivated by profit; a shared interest, passion, skills match or new experience can be the driving motivation. Indeed, participants only participate as long as they realise value. It may earn them money, help address an issue they need to tackle, allow them to do something they're passionate about, or help to achieve more than would otherwise be possible.

In the quest for a substantial improvement in resource performance across the economy, businesses have started to explore ways to reuse products or their components and restore more of their precious material, energy and labour inputs. **It's a step towards what's being called the "circular economy" – replacing the dominant "take-make-dispose" pattern with much greater levels of systemic reuse and recycling and elimination of waste.** The idea of "consumers" is replaced with that of "users", with manufacturers taking back their products after use, thus encouraging a massive shift in the interest and activity of efficient reuse and recycling. Recent work has indicated this shift could yield annual net material cost savings of at least US$380 billion, just for a subset of the European manufacturing sectors. Beyond material savings, there are also benefits of mitigating material volatility and supply risks, additional employment opportunities, reduced externalities and overall longer-term resilience of the economy.[25]

25 Ellen Macarthur Foundation (2013) *Towards the circular economy – economic and business rationale for an accelerated transition*, EMF, Isle of Wight, UK

Take the example

We helped a mining company to identify a business-to-business collaboration as one of a suite of solutions to manage air emissions which had reached the regulated emissions level and had thus become a severe constraint on growth in their operations.

The client was frustrated that technical solutions to control dust and other emissions seemed to have been exhausted, preventing further mineral export through their ports. To remove this constraint cost-effectively, we identified an opportunity to collaborate with smaller, adjacent competitors. It would involve investing in reducing their emissions; with their collaborators' agreement they could effectively "buy" the resulting improvement in the local air quality and increase their regulated emissions limit.

Uncommon practice

Does a high level of advocacy for collaboration translate into corresponding practice on the ground? In our opinion and in the context of the way we are conceiving collaboration, the answer to this question is "no". Furthermore, it's important to understand why, as a first step in remedying this situation.

It seems that many organisations involved in developing and operating infrastructure are still evolving in their approach to stakeholder engagement and collaboration. The most basic stakeholder relationship (particularly as it relates to new policies or projects) can be described as "decide and defend", where the organisation holds the view that its approach is right and that with adequate information, the reasonable stakeholders will come to agree.

More developed approaches to stakeholder involvement and collaboration involve listening to the views of others to obtain a fuller exchange of views and information, but with the initiating organisation still controlling the scope and decisions, which effectively limits the creative input of prospective partners. This is the realm in which corporate responsibility and community investments can often reside – where organisations contribute to communities as a form of "aid" but the core business direction and associated projects are not materially influenced by the stakeholders.

Collaborative Spectrum

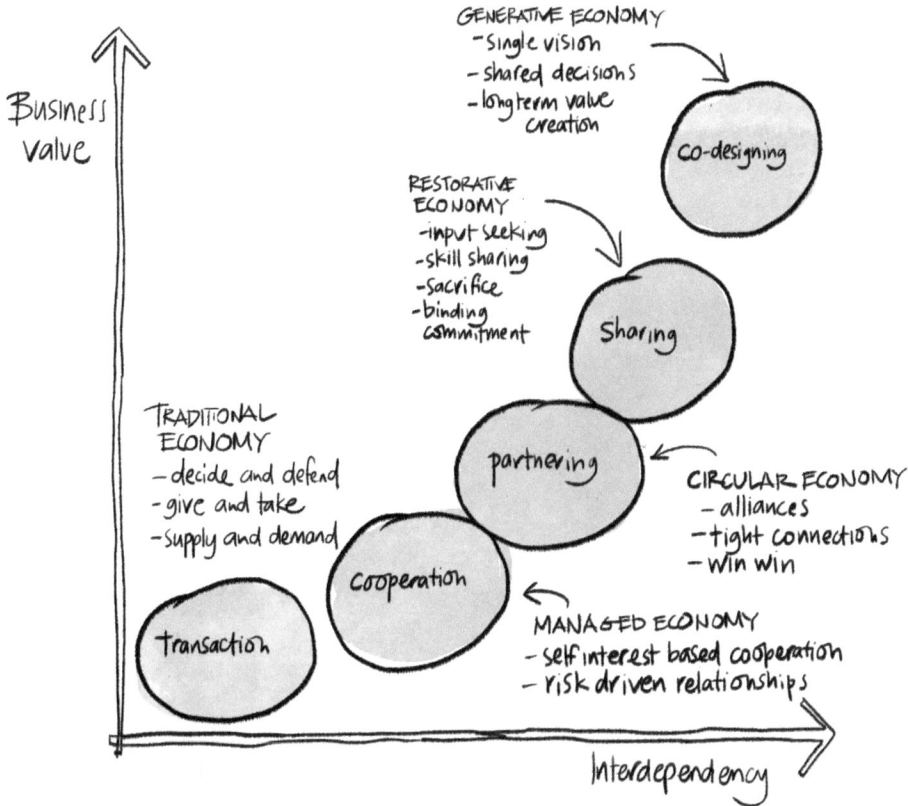

Business value

GENERATIVE ECONOMY
- single vision
- shared decisions
- long term value creation

Co-designing

RESTORATIVE ECONOMY
- input seeking
- skill sharing
- sacrifice
- binding commitment

Sharing

TRADITIONAL ECONOMY
- decide and defend
- give and take
- supply and demand

partnering

CIRCULAR ECONOMY
- alliances
- tight connections
- win win

cooperation

MANAGED ECONOMY
- self interest based cooperation
- risk driven relationships

transaction

Interdependency

Many of the dominant forms of collaboration are driven by traditional self-interest (cooperation and partnering). "Enlightened self-interest" can drive higher forms of collaboration where the input of other stakeholders is sought – at its highest level to co-design and co-deliver assets, products and services that create long-term value for the leading organisation as well as society.

True collaboration sits at the other end of the spectrum, where the "system is brought into the room" through representative stakeholders. For example, for a major infrastructure project, the stakeholders might include people involved along the project life cycle (from financiers, designers and constructors to operators) as well as those affected by or with the potential to affect the project (including regulators, local government officials, and residents). The purpose is, of course, to co-develop an agreed project and development pathway that will gain stakeholder support and therefore be as efficient, useful and enduring as possible.

Take the example We know some people will view this collaborative approach as impractical, but we've seen it produce great results, including for one particular power company. The utility was undertaking public consultation in the approvals phase of the largest transmission line project undertaken in its state for 20 years. Lack of community support had become a serious business issue that affected new projects as well as ongoing maintenance. The proposed transmission line had the very real potential to provoke negative community reaction, create major delays, incur additional costs and further erode the company's social licence. The utility fully intended to consult with stakeholders, but also assumed a conventional "decide and defend" approach. We managed to convince them to consider a different path and to re-frame the project challenge as "How can we assess alignment options and identify the best route, as well as build community support and trust through the process?"

So instead of explaining their plans to stakeholders and defending their rationale and decision, the utility's managers sat down with people living along the transmission line corridor to talk about their interests, needs and places of value. By mapping that information, new insights and many more cost-effective route options emerged that preserved stakeholders' needs and values. In effect, the utility had engaged in a form of "co-design".

The results went way beyond what was thought possible, saving $US2million and shaving 2 years from the project timetable:
• No community objections were lodged (a very surprising result for this type of project).
• The government deemed that an EIA was no longer required.

The project's approach was recognised in several Excellence Awards, and turned what could have been an adversarial process into one that built trust along with the company's social licence.

This type of real collaboration is still relatively rare. It represents a real shift in attitude and behaviour from business as usual, and therein lies a key barrier to change. Change brings all the usual challenges, and old habits die slowly.

The motivation to change can also be a problem. Many organisations fear community engagement, holding a strong belief that it will be a negative and adversarial experience through which they may lose control of both the process and associated information. To an extent this is borne of the "decide and defend" approach and a long history of NIMBYism ("not in my back yard!") and special interest group opposition to development projects, which in some respects appears to be escalating. Indeed, perpetuating the "decide and defend" approach to stakeholder engagement in development projects is unlikely to generate any other response. It's a self-fulfilling prophecy that needn't occur.

Of course, the tenor of stakeholder relationships can be heightened for infrastructure and utility businesses because they typically provide essential services and are highly visible, networked and embedded in society; unlike consumer products firms that consumers can choose to have a relationship with, we are all stakeholders in efficient power, gas, transport, telecommunications and water services. As such, these organisations have many diverse stakeholders who desire inclusion in the decision-making process. This has the potential to make the stakeholder interactions highly charged, and it's understandable why many attempt to avoid them.

Business executives and project managers who have engaged in more collaborative business and project delivery arrangements report that the greatest difficulties for sustaining them include cultural differences between the collaborating parties and agreeing on appropriate risk and reward allocations. Having said this, the general view of these managers is that reverting to previous, more adversarial ways of working is not an option any more, and is likely to increase the risks and negative outcomes.[26]

26 MBS (2009) Study on voluntary arrangements for collaboration in construction, Final report, Part 2: best practice guide and case studies, Manchester Business School, University of Manchester

Who do you collaborate with?

Who are the stakeholders in your business or project? Do you understand their interests, level of influence over your success, and what merit there may be in developing closer, collaborative relationships?

It can be remarkably revealing to think about what success would look like for a stakeholder, and how it might be feasible to meet their needs or aspirations as well as your own. It can also help reveal what you know and don't know – thus providing a basis for identifying potential collaborators.

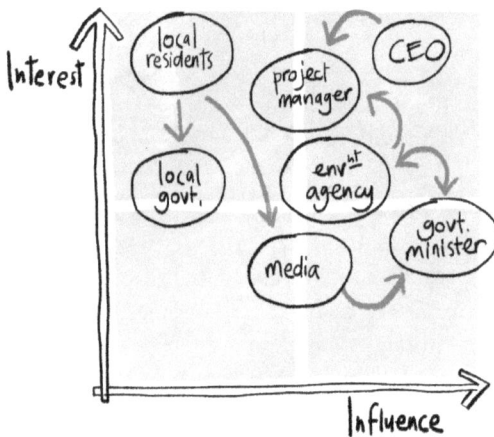

Often many different stakeholders will have an interest in a project or organisation. Failure to recognise their interests can create major risks. While they may not have substantial direct influence over project or business success, they may magnify their influence via relationships with other stakeholders. These risks can often be overcome, and translated into real project and business value, by finding ways to proactively address stakeholder concerns and desires. Bringing stakeholders into a co-design and decision-making process can be very effective.

Take the example

A major inner-city arterial road upgrade provides an interesting example. The project team was focused on the engineering design and delivery task of increasing the through-put capacity of a relatively short section of road. When opening the discussion to talk about stakeholders, local councils were recognised mainly because they would need to be advised and involved in managing any inconvenience when the expected construction activities commenced. But the conversation quickly turned when we asked: "*What would success look like for the local councils?*" The arterial road formed the boundary line separating two council areas. Each had a different local traffic management policy and it became clear the councils might actually be contributing to the problem, and might even make it worse in future. The congestion problems were really the consequence of traffic management decisions made in the wider road system, in which the councils were important players. All of a sudden, this was not just an engineering design and delivery project. It was a facilitation and negotiation project.

Collaborating successfully

So what does it take to collaborate successfully?

First and foremost, business or project leaders must recognise a reason to collaborate. Without perceived benefits and a commitment to putting effort into collaboration it will simply fail.

Leaders must recognise that existing organisational culture, structure and processes may need to change to accommodate the pursuit of value that is offered via collaboration. So a critical ingredient is **leadership** – to explain the benefits of collaboration, to role-model collaborative mindsets and behaviour, and to reward aligned effort and achievement.

Shared interests and complementary objectives are further important ingredients. People must see and derive value if they are to enter into and sustain a partnership. This involves everyone being clear and transparent about their **objectives** – what they want from the collaboration, what they think they can provide, and what they expect to get from others.

Similar transparency about the ethics and values that will be adopted by the collaborating parties is required. **Trust** and respect is *absolutely pivotal* to creating an environment in which parties are prepared to openly share information and "give and take" in achieving the over-arching goals. This point cannot be over-stated. So a preparedness to be transparent and behave consistently with agreed principles provides a good start and a solid foundation.

With these building blocks in place, it's important to ensure the team is **aligned**. It's not enough to have the business or project leader's commitment if progress can be thwarted, undermined or under-realised by people who don't share that commitment. So "getting the right people on the bus" is another key ingredient. This means carefully selecting both the collaborating organisations *and* the specific people from those organisations.

Consistent with spirit and purpose of collaboration is **shared decision making**, which can be a challenging path to walk. To collaborate effectively, people must feel and experience a capacity to influence decisions. So shared decision making involves parties voluntarily giving up some of their benefit or control for a better net result for all parties, recognising that there will always be a party with greater authority and the expectation of making a final decision. It demands flexibility in approach to achieve mutual benefit without compromising fundamental principles or objectives.

Frequent and **transparent communication, monitoring and review** of progress will keep the collaboration on track and focused on its shared objectives as well as responding to areas of departure. How these issues are addressed is secondary to (a) generating enthusiasm and reinforcing commitment through a sense of progress, and (b) knowing where the problems lie and where the power of the collaborating parties and their collective talents can be targeted to resolve the problems.

Consistent with this process of monitoring and review, there's a need to recognise that **failures** can and will occur along the way. This needs to be recognised and accepted as a valuable learning experience – a signpost on the road to future success.

Rewards for effort and achievement are important in any process involving mindset and behaviour change, no less in collaborative ventures. As mentioned above, the rewards may be financial in nature but need not always be so, as collaborating stakeholders may not be financially motivated (such as the landholders participating in the planning and siting of high voltage power lines).

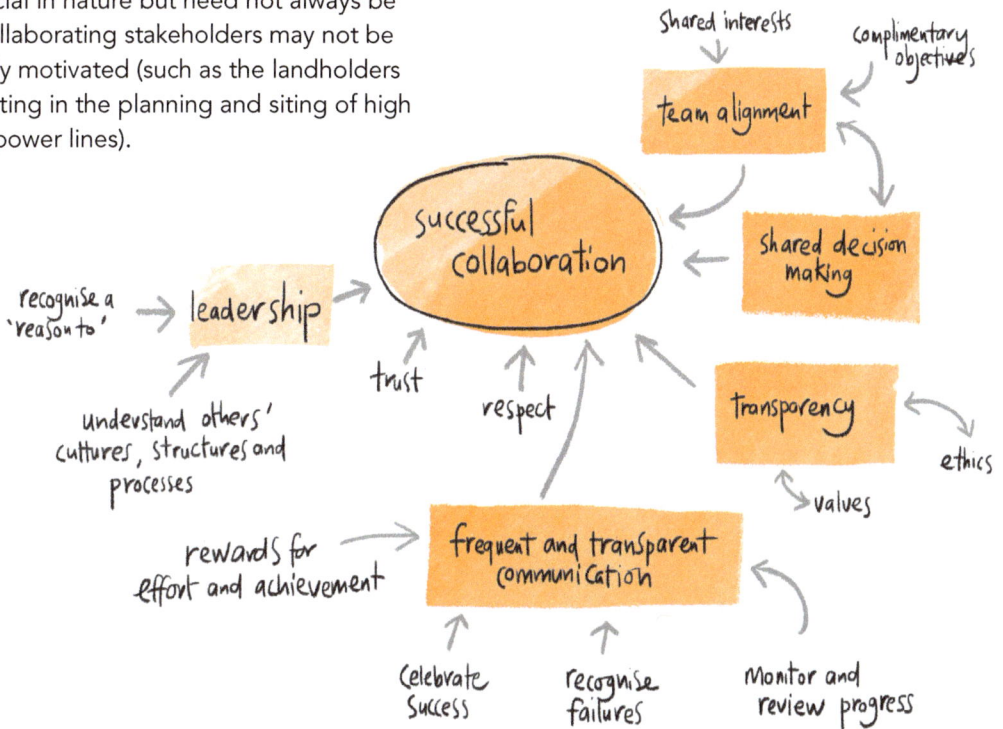

shared interests

complimentary objectives

team alignment

shared decision making

successful collaboration

recognise a 'reason to'

leadership

understand others' cultures, structures and processes

trust

respect

transparency

ethics

values

rewards for effort and achievement

frequent and transparent communication

Celebrate Success

recognise failures

Monitor and review progress

A growing evidence base shows that the organisations that put the effort into understanding their stakeholders and involve them in co-design and co-management (creating shared value) will be the organisations that survive and thrive. This means shifting away from an efficiency and competition-dominated operating model to collaborate with purpose when it makes sense.

The future belongs to those who collaborate

Business conditions and societal demands compel infrastructure providers and utilities to find ways to deploy under-utilised assets, to find new, and unique applications for assets, or to employ or combine assets to create new discrete sources of value to ensure they are low-risk and high-value throughout their establishment and operating phases.

This shift in business practice, as with many others discussed earlier in this book, is entirely achievable. Yet it often means making a material change from business-as-usual practices. This is where a coach can be very helpful. Just as an athlete benefits from the performance analysis, skill training, perspective and encouragement of a coach, so can a project or business team. So what does it take to be that coach and add real value? We explore this in the next few chapters.

USEFUL QUESTIONS

- **Do you know what really matters to stakeholders who can influence your success?**

- **Who could you collaborate with to achieve even greater benefits and outcomes?**

- **Are you prepared to demonstrate leadership, transparency and sharing of decision making to make collaboration work?**

Nine

Delivering the project vision

A vision is not a result.

Outcomes need a focus on action.

Without the will to change, nothing new happens.

"Vision without action is a daydream. Action without vision is a nightmare."

Japanese proverb

Take the example

"The best intentions were there at the start – but the demands of schedule and delivery really became the focus."

This comment came from a senior engineer managing a major port development project. It was really an apology to us, as he tried to explain why his team had not pursued their "best intentions". What could have happened to compromise the "best" intentions of the team? During the planning stages of the project, we'd helped the team develop exciting and achievable project objectives and targets for sustainable development to reduce costs, build community trust and navigate a complex approvals process – which would generate major and lasting benefits for the project owner, the organisation and the community. The project owner and team supported and were enthusiastic about the challenge and sense of what was possible. However, when we conducted an audit a year into the project, we found it was falling far short of the original sustainability vision and goals. Although we had worked with the team to establish an achievable sustainability platform for the project, our role finished at that point – and we were not embedded in the project team for the work that followed. So what happened?

This is what happened. Sustainable outcomes are not typically "business as usual" or more of the same. They require us to do something differently. This "something" involves setting a vision and specific objectives, and developing genuine solutions that contribute to lasting wellbeing. It shifts the focus from reducing the impacts of development to designing for long-term benefits. It requires us to re-frame the problem and look beyond the project site for solutions, and work not just for efficient solutions (with only incremental improvement) but for solutions that actually *change things for the better, for the long-term*. It takes a commitment and energy which can be hard to initiate, let alone sustain with a set of deliverables looming. Reverting to previously tried and true practices is the easier and more predictable path. That's what happened with the senior engineer delivering the major port development. It wasn't that the demands of "schedule and delivery" became the focus. They'd always been the focus. What happened was that he and his team *lost their focus* on actions to achieve the "best" intentions they set for their project.

The gap

So what does it take to actually operationalise and implement the intent to achieve sustainable outcomes, to "make it happen" and translate it into a project's design and delivery? It's true that a compelling vision and strong strategy are fundamental pillars for successful projects and time should always be spent on them – but a vision and strategy are worth little without purposeful execution. Developing a project vision or goal that is a stretch, but achievable doesn't mean it will then somehow just "happen". It takes effort and a good process, and you need to stay focused on the effort. Particularly if the goal requires you to do something differently to attain it.

Change is difficult, requires effort and carries risk, which is why most people tend to avoid it. Having someone to carry the load and coach change along the way makes it a lot more palatable, less risky and more likely to stick. It also makes being involved in change process a stimulating and even enjoyable experience.

Integration is similar in many ways. *How* does integration occur not just on a superficial level, but on the fundamental and most material issues? Adding or combining is often mistaken for integrating, whereas integration is really about collaborating to assimilate different elements or ideas for a more unified and whole solution. It's more than the sum of the parts.

Just about all the organisations that deliver major infrastructure projects have a sustainability vision agreed at Board or executive level. Where we see some of the best fall short is their lack of an effective process for systematically translating

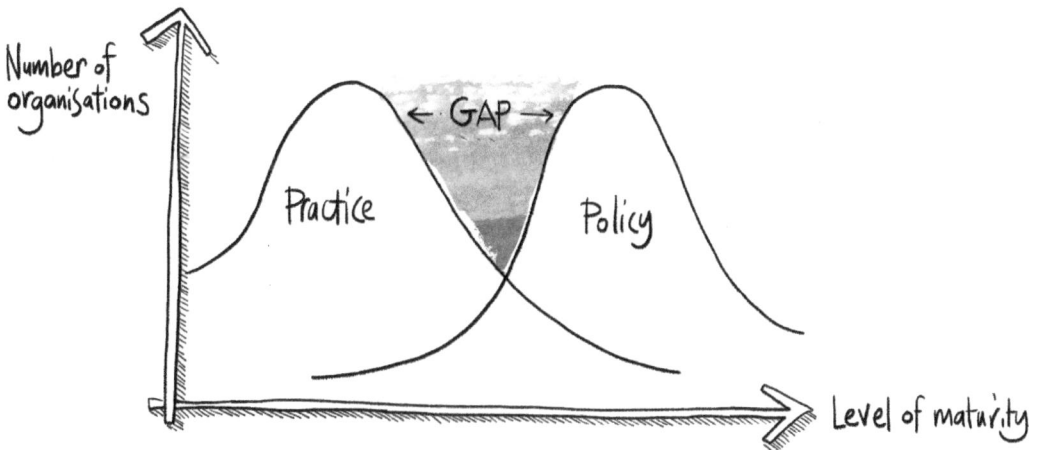

their sustainability vision and goals into practical language and action. When an organisation genuinely connects its vision and strategy with its on-ground delivery, the results are immensely powerful – but we typically see the potential of sustainable opportunities unrealised by many, even by the organisations considered as "leaders in their field".

It's often called the "policy–practice gap" and it's very real for mature global organisations and government agencies as well as smaller businesses (although they are reluctant to recognise it). This gap manifests itself in many ways – including in relevant language, lack of a practical roadmap for action, or little agreement on what success will look like in tangible terms.

Language is at the heart of good communication. Strategy or policy is usually expressed in aspirational terms, with high-level guiding principles and concepts. Common sustainability-related language familiar to many includes "maintaining social licence", "building community capacity" and "maintaining liveability". These

are very worthy goals – but unless a way is found to translate them into tangible and operational expressions of action that someone really owns and can act upon, they will not be achieved. Organisations must connect them to a project's approach and all its activities.

Decisions and action are needed. Which individuals and teams will focus on achieving the sustainability goals? When and how should their work be integrated into other project streams? How are teams going to collaborate on smarter solutions?

This is what a "sustainability manager" does. Innovation, integration, external affairs, strategy or sustainability manager – the title may vary, but the role is needed and its tasks remain the same.

Our consistent experience is that without someone active in such a role, the initial impetus and energy to achieve an exciting vision is gradually lost due to the pressures on delivery, the complexity of projects and project teams, and the energy it takes to initiate change and, most importantly, to see it through.

Making the vision happen

Sustainability managers help translate policy into practice to deliver better outcomes for organisations and projects. They take the sustainable vision of a project then design and facilitate a structured way to collaborate for integrated and more effective solutions. A lot of their activities involve facilitating and coaching a project team to connect multiple disciplines so the vision is integrated into all tasks. They ask and respond to the questions:
What do we need to do differently?
What will be this project's positive legacy?
Will it have any negative legacies?
What assumptions should be challenged?

We find these questions stimulating but we've learned they can challenge even the most experienced professionals. It's not necessarily that they don't want to achieve better outcomes. It's because nobody has worked with them to see it through. Because of this, they can see the questions as risks, not opportunities. This was clearly evident in a project manager we once worked with, who was grappling with incorporating his organisation's corporate objectives into his project. One objective was: "Net positive impact on biodiversity". He asked us: "*What does it even mean? How do I go about implementing this?*" Typically this query is forgotten in the fast pace of capital project design and delivery – especially if it requires the team to do something differently. A sustainability manager works with the team to reframe the problem and challenge the thinking to develop different solutions.

So <u>whose</u> role is it to deliver the vision? I'm sure it's not on the schedule of deliverables

The value of persistence

Success in the role of sustainability and innovation requires persistence and follow-through. Without it, nothing changes.

This was our experience in the early design of a large desalination plant. The process of desalination generates bio-sludge, and there were real opportunities to provide this as a raw material for particular industries instead of transporting it to landfill as usually happens. It would take some effort to gain support from the relevant regulatory agencies and to promote the product to the market but it was all very practical and achievable; the financial and other benefits were obvious and we knew others had done the same and achieved success. But it represented change. Without a champion in the management team to drive that change, the idea lost momentum, failed to progress and the opportunity was lost.

We love being asked if what we do is "worthwhile" because it's easy to answer, as we experience and hear so many positive outcomes about the value of working for sustainable results. Duncan, the project manager of a team delivering an inner-urban busway transport corridor that included several new stations, related what happened the first time a sustainability manager joined his project team: "*The person in this role needed persistence because in hindsight all the team wanted to do was to get on with the job. One challenge we had was the houses located in the corridor, which had to be removed. We just wanted to do what we always did – which meant demolishing 30 homes. The sustainability manager consistently challenged this thinking and persisted with the team – and in the end we didn't demolish any houses at all. Just 16 houses were affected and we re-located all of them. It meant 60 per cent less waste to landfill and it demonstrated that we'd given serious thought in our decisions for better community and environmental outcomes. Plus, the team felt really good about what they'd achieved, and saw first-hand the benefits of thinking 'outside the box', and it motivated them to keep on with it.*"

Fostering innovation

Many organisations and project managers seek innovation, but few have a robust, structured process to genuinely foster it. Many believe the action of starting an "innovation register" on their intranet makes them innovative. Over the years, we've seen numerous innovation registers launched by organisations and they often become the yardstick to assess the calibre, extent and impact of an organisation's innovation culture. But a good portion of these registers do little more than record individual ideas connected in some way to innovation. While these have some value, they don't initiate collaboration, or give the necessary focus or structure to the priority issues and are often just a collection of disparate, good ideas.

Innovation is really a "team sport". To cultivate a genuinely collaborative and innovative culture, a more systematic approach to innovation that "starts at the start" of a project is needed to connect disciplines, take a step back, facilitate a collaborative process and target most effort on the genuine challenges. This is the role of a sustainability manager.

Sometimes it's the approach of a sustainability manager to a project that makes the difference. A colleague of ours, Alistair, manages innovation and sustainable development on complex integrated urban development projects.

When the government of the day began pressing for rapid residential development of a large urban greenfield site, Alistair knew he had a problem because it can take 3 years to complete just the planning and approvals process. He decided on a different approach, which involved all stakeholders – the local government, state government utilities, developers, community groups, and Indigenous groups – contributing to design up-front in a fully integrated and hands-on process. All disciplines on the design team were involved, and with the help of graphic artists Alistair continually provided visual evidence to show community members and organisations how their input and suggestions were being incorporated into the design as discussions progressed. The momentum and consensus this generated achieved the extraordinary result of approval gained for the whole process in less than 9 months – more than a year ahead of the tight schedule. The result was a better design that had strong support from all significant stakeholder groups, so there were fewer delays. Alistair's alternative was an avalanche of community objections and low stakeholder support that could have held his project up for years.

It was the up-front investment in a fully collaborative process designed and driven by the sustainability manager and involving all disciplines and stakeholders that won success for the project.

Take the example

A colleague likes to explain "what he does" by relating his experience managing innovation and sustainability on a major urban rail project. He was presented with work the team had already done, which consisted of 280 separate ideas captured on the innovation register. What was he to do with this? Were all the ideas worthy innovations that deserved investigation and action? His first step was to re-position the initiative as "innovation with purpose" – that is, to connect it with the critical project objectives. A simple framework was developed with the team that structured and prioritised the 280 ideas around three criteria: to be considered further, an idea had to be cost effective and adaptable for future needs, and it had to support sustainable urban growth.

This structure helped consolidate and structure the long list of individual ideas in terms of core opportunities. A number of ideas were developed into real and substantive solutions across the project. Without our colleague and team working on a more thoughtful approach to innovation, none of these solutions would have happened – and yet the benefits achieved were staggering. Over 35 per cent of the initial US$800 million project budget was saved (US$290 million) without materially changing the project scope. That surprised just about everyone.

This remarkable success was achieved by consolidating and focusing innovation effort on the most significant challenges, and identifying powerful connections between formerly disparate ideas. For example, the team reconsidered the standard tunnel design for the large number of road and rail crossings in the project and, after asking a few questions, identified a better and more efficient design. This saved the equivalent of seven Olympic-sized swimming pools of high-quality structural concrete – without compromising quality or functionality. So one sustainability manager working with the team achieved all these benefits and saved US$290 million. Worthwhile results for everyone through more purposeful innovation.

Being, and staying, motivated

We've found that a key part of our role in driving sustainable development is maintaining a high level of motivation and even inspiration across a project team or organisation. This can play out in all sorts of ways. Duncan related an example of how this worked on the busway transport corridor we mentioned above. Someone, probably a commuter, called the project office one day and yelled: "*So where are we supposed to put our bikes?*" and hung up. Ordinarily, the team would have dismissed the call, as the need for cost reductions had seen bike storage facilities cut from the project scope. But there was a spirit and culture of responding to all challenges and finding better solutions, so the team returned to thinking about bike storage. Not long after, 60 bike lockers were installed at the new stations, paid for from the substantial savings the project achieved – US$2 million under budget and 6 months ahead of schedule.

These savings were partly due to the culture of innovation and striving for better outcomes the sustainability manager and team had cultivated throughout the project.

Working across silos

While the problems that arise from teams working in organisational silos are well known, it's much less recognised as a risk within large project teams. When a project is big, we often find a lack of integration between task teams, disciplines and environmental and engineering design work as well as social planners and procurement. If integration is attempted at all, it's usually perfunctory, or at the end of the design process.

Sustainability managers bring different thinking to your project. They think in connected systems rather than isolated elements. Their thinking style is to "join the dots", which means they're not focused on a single task or element like most other team members, but on the whole project and its wider context. They aren't necessarily looking for a single discipline to provide the "best" solution. Their role is to foster genuine collaboration and shared thinking between disciplines and build a more connected perspective, which is often new to project teams. We've seen many teams surprised with the results they've achieved with input from a professional skilled at integrating ideas and actions from design to delivery.

A colleague of ours, Frank, describes his role as *"getting the thoughtful and stimulating conversations going across teams and tasks"*. Frank was providing sustainability advice to a 20-year urban regeneration project in the United Kingdom. The project would see a derelict inner city area transformed into a new business park that would eventually house over 1,000 media-related businesses. Frank believes a critical early decision he made was to facilitate "mini-conversations" across the project's different disciplines. This provided the platform for all his subsequent successes. These mini-conversations were sometimes informal and casual. They aimed to stimulate and capture everyone's ideas about how to resolve the big issues with smarter and more sustainable solutions.
Frank credits them as the catalyst that generated the project's subsequent recognition as a flagship development and global centre of excellence.

Just one of the inspired and integrated solutions that Frank achieved with his mini-conversations was a tri-generation energy scheme developed as a "total asset". This involved managing energy in an integrated way across the whole site for heating, cooling and energy generation, rather than developing a series of separate solutions. In addition to heating and cooling the business premises more reliably and efficiently for a much lower cost, greenhouse gas emissions were reduced and valuable land on the urban site was freed up for other uses. Working in siloed teams would not have produced this outcome. The mini-conversations that Frank engineered triggered greater connection across the project team that challenged accepted practice to generate transformative innovation and genuine sustainable development.

Silo approach

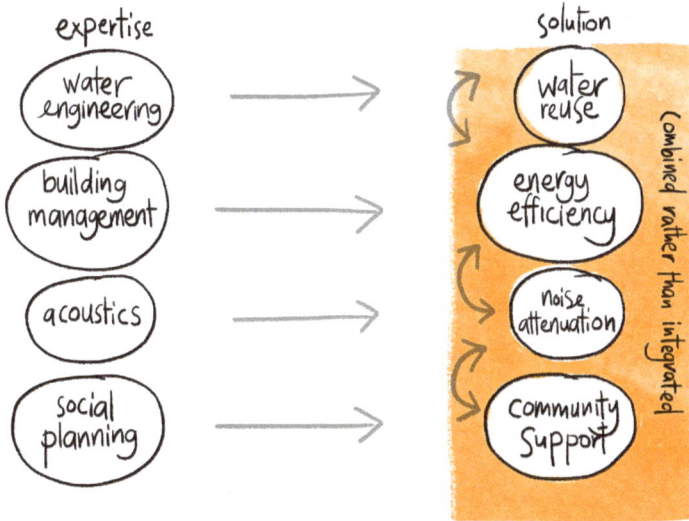

expertise

- water engineering
- building management
- acoustics
- social planning

Solution

- water reuse
- energy efficiency
- noise attenuation
- community support

Combined rather than integrated

People often think that "working collaboratively" means working as part of a common team, joining together the solutions from individual functions or disciplines. We argue in favour of working together in a more integrated way, and thinking systemically together before developing solutions together.

Collaborative approach

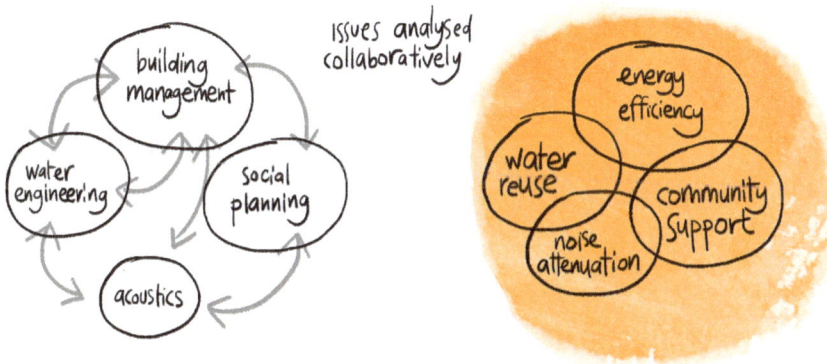

- building management
- water engineering
- social planning
- acoustics

issues analysed collaboratively

- energy efficiency
- water reuse
- community support
- noise attenuation

Demonstrating value

This role in organisations and on projects is still relatively new and we often find many project teams have little idea of not just its structure, tasks and outputs, but also of its value. It's easy to discount the value offered before experiencing what it can achieve. Two common arguments we hear against a dedicated sustainability or innovation manager on a project are: *"But the project manager and technical designers deliver integration and innovation so why do we need another person?"* and *"We don't think a sustainability expert can deliver substantial benefits for this particular project."* We disagree on both counts.

Firstly, project managers and technical designers are focused and fully occupied in delivery according to the set project scope and schedule. Their focus is not to seek different, innovative solutions and re-think assumptions. They judge acceptable solutions through the lens of past practice in their technical discipline and training, which doesn't encourage them to consider issues holistically and identify all the interconnections.

As one of our most experienced project managers said: "Project managers manage. They are focused on delivering against the agreed project scope and schedule, and doing that takes all of their time. They may value and support integration, innovation and collaboration and better solutions, but they won't initiate, drive and facilitate a process to deliver on them."

Secondly, an effective sustainability manager achieves multiple benefits for any project and the investment in them is quickly repaid many times over – in our particular profession the repayment comes in the form of better project design. Better design can generate massive savings in time and increase the efficiency of the projects we work on, as well as building social licence and reputation.

Of course, projects operate within an organisational culture and setting. This has a big effect on what has a realistic chance of success. How do you make sustainability an organisational strategy that sticks? We'll delve into this further in the next chapter.

USEFUL QUESTIONS

- **What silos have you experienced within projects or organisations? What effect did they have?**

- **How does real integration occur in your projects on the issues that matter most?**

- **What is the current approach to fostering innovation directed at the most material challenges or issues?**

- **How would you ensure that an exciting vision for an initiative is fully realised and implemented?**

Ten

Making the strategy stick

Bridging the gap between policy and practice is all about strategy execution.

Strategy execution involves leading and managing change.

Leadership, resource allocation and alignment of effort are crucial to success.

"In real life, strategy is actually
very straightforward.
You pick a general direction
and implement like hell."

Jack Welch in *Winning*, 2005

"There's no difference between our business strategy and a sustainability strategy – at least there shouldn't be."

Chief Financial Officer of a major utility

The senior executive quoted above made this comment to us while reflecting on the changing business landscape and the economic, social and environmental factors his business had to address to maintain its success.

Of course it's true for all organisations in some shape or form.

Yet how do you translate sustainability risks and opportunities into a tangible agenda and actions that provide a meaningful return on investment, particularly at a time when the challenge for business leaders and their organisations to "do more with less" has never been greater?

Impediments to progress

It's really quite clear that sustainability is an umbrella term for a suite of issues that are of direct strategic importance to business and civil governance. Why then has it taken so long for organisational leaders to recognise this and respond?

We believe there are a number of reasons. Firstly, share markets have tended to reward short-term profit-seeking behaviour, particularly in publicly traded companies driven by quarterly earnings reports. The same basic instinct to avoid risks and satisfy desires for immediate gratification has similarly influenced the agenda of governments, many of which find themselves in increasingly tenuous political and economic circumstances that further reinforce a short-term view. This translates into a second and related cause, which is a lack of strategic foresight or a limited capacity to exercise that foresight. In essence, these factors have a common root cause: the absence of genuine leadership.

A third cause of reluctance to engage with sustainability is the persistence of a strong narrative connecting sustainability with a "deep green" environmental and political movement, placing sustainability at the fringe both in business and in political communities. While this is no longer the case for the more enlightened and progressive businesses, it is true that the leadership of many organisations still sees sustainability issues as environmental in nature, likely to be addressed through regulation and "green tape", and thus something to be opposed as an increased business cost and avoided until the last moment. The risk and opportunity are perceived to be too small to motivate action, with little or no short-term return on investment.

Then there is the personal brand risk. Which senior executive is happy to risk being seen as not having had their finger on the pulse, understanding their business risks and opportunities, or worse yet, being regarded by their peers as a "tree-hugging greenie"? (Of course, equally few wish to be branded as an environmental or social butcher!)

Of course exceptions exist – in the form of entrepreneurs creating small start-up businesses that respond to gaps in the market, or intrapreneurs[27] with the commercial acumen and social intelligence to survive and thrive in large organisations (see Chapter 11 for more on the role of sustainability managers).

Business leaders cannot duck and hide these issues for much longer. The assumptions of the past are being severely challenged. Business strategists can no longer rely on a world that has an endless supply of resources, cheap fossil fuels, a benign climate and limitless capacity to absorb waste, where consumer demand and economies grow forever, enabled by cheap credit. That landscape will never return. Key factors once treated as externalities now need to be considered. Increasingly, business executives who don't seek to understand and respond to the risks and opportunities will be regarded as unfit to lead, and their organisations as unfit to fund, insure, buy from or work for.

27 Intrapreneur: a person who while remaining within a larger organization uses entrepreneurial skills to develop a new product or line of business as a subsidiary of the organisation

Accenture and UNGP[28] surveyed some of the world's leading CEOs to explore their ideas and actions on sustainability. They found strong confidence and growing evidence that sustainable business practices were possible – 81 per cent of the CEOs reported that sustainability issues were now fully embedded into the strategy and operations of their company, compared with just 50 per cent three years earlier in 2007.

However, this had not permeated into all elements of core business—that is, into capabilities, processes and systems. There is a significant performance gap between those CEOs who agree that sustainability should be embedded throughout their subsidiaries (91 per cent) and supply chain (88 per cent), and those who report that their company is already doing so (59 per cent and 54 per cent, respectively).

Similarly, company directors will be regarded as unfit to govern because long-term value creation, the oversight of strategy and risk, and legal compliance, are their primary fiduciary responsibilities.

Bridging the policy-practice gap

So how do you make sustainability real, meaningful and warranting action? In conceptual terms the task is quite straightforward. Organisations need to agree on why action on sustainability is required, what should be done, and how best to implement those actions and initiatives. In practice it is somewhat more complicated, not just for the reasons outlined above. There is ample evidence, even from leading organisations, that translating policies into practice is challenging. We call this the challenge of the "policy–practice gap".

This was confirmed in a recent study by Ethical Corporation involving research and in-depth interviews with C-level executives of leading multi-national companies. Just one-third of organisations were delivering on their corporate responsibility goals. The remaining two-thirds were largely "just starting out" or "working on it". Further, issue identification (or materiality assessment) and setting of goals and targets were the areas where organisations were most progressed. Translating that into an implementation roadmap was very much a work in progress and required more attention.

While there is no one-size-fits-all response, we have found the following approaches useful in client organisations as well as our own.

28 Accenture, UNGC (2010) *A new era of sustainability*, UN Global Compact-Accenture CEO Study.

Get beyond green and philanthropy

If sustainability is to gain traction and provide benefits to an organisation, it must be understood in the Board room and C-suite. There's a need to get beyond "green" as the primary interpretation of sustainability. As outlined earlier in this book, we have found that engaging people in dialogue about the current and emerging challenges is a quick and effective way of transcending a discussion about the environment, making it one about the inter-related forces shaping our economies, societies and environment. Fundamentally the conversation can shift to what it will take for an organisation to remain viable, relevant and "fit for the future" within that changing context. For design intent is important not only to projects but also to our enterprises. For an organisation to be sustainable, we need to *want* it to be. As we observe in our own organisation, "profit is like blood in the body – it's necessary for life but not the reason for living".

Assess materiality

Sustainability is an umbrella term for a wide range of inter-related issues, aspirations and opportunities. It can trigger a vast array of responses which can be overwhelming and confusing. So it's important to clarify what aspects are relevant for an organisation to address at any point in time and to focus on as the most important or "material".

A comparison of two studies by SustainAbility[29] showed that emerging market companies focus more on short-term cost savings and revenue gains, while intangibles like brand value and reputational issues are more significant in developed countries. Community investment and development are seen primarily as an overhead in developed countries, but in emerging markets they are shown to be important in retaining the licence to operate and in reducing risk.

If approached from a risk perspective, the level of risk (consequence and likelihood) and ability to address that risk are two simple parameters that can be used to undertake a rapid appraisal of matters on which to focus.

When undertaking a materiality assessment, it's also useful to look up and down the supply chain to understand the market forces at play and the stakeholders involved, otherwise there's a risk that important issues will be missed. What matters to your customers, staff and suppliers should be of interest to you too.

---

29 SustainAbility and International Finance Corporation (2002)
Developing Value: The business case for sustainability in emerging markets, SustainAbility Ltd, London

The materiality of financial, ethical, workforce, environmental and social issues is assessed by looking at the risk issues pose to business and the degree to which they are important to stakeholders. When coupled with consideration of the timing of these risks, this simple matrix becomes a useful tool in prioritising effort to enhance the sustainability of the enterprise in a way that engages business stakeholders.

(Adapted from materiality assessment conducted by DeBeers in 2010)

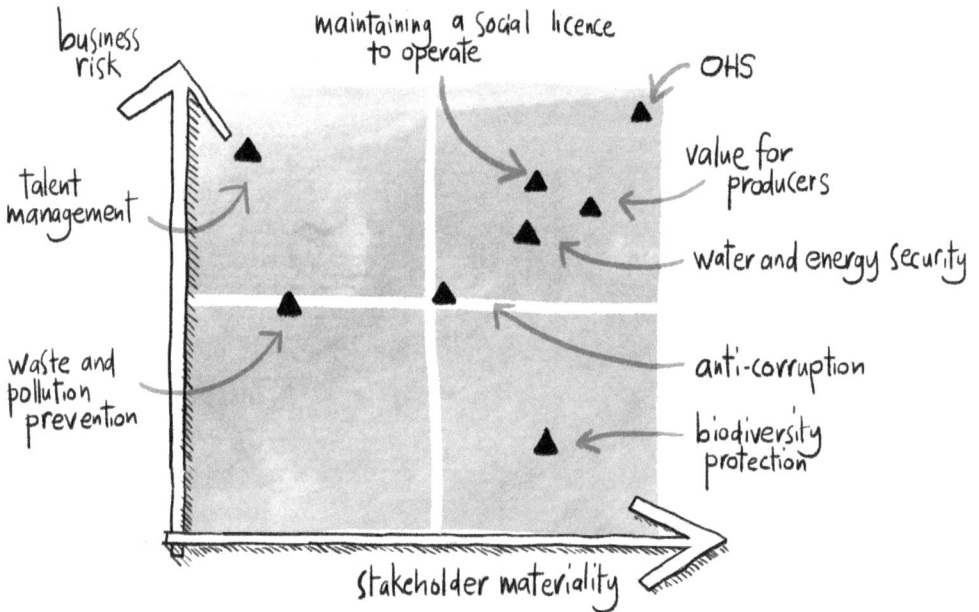

Grow in maturity

Being "fit for the future" will mean different things to different organisations, even those operating in the same geographic region and market sector, and will be influenced by the culture and risk appetite of an organisation. For some, it will mean maintaining legal compliance with evolving regulations. Other organisations will regard "fitness" as an ability to respond to changing regulatory and customer requirements, as well as to shape the market to create competitive advantage. However, because these market shapers always exist, those that regard "compliance" as sufficient arguably put their organisations at risk and are likely to fail to create enduring value for their organisations, shareholders and customers.

Indeed, a leading international authority on company and competitive strategy, Michael Porter, suggests that to survive and thrive, organisations must be creating "shared value". Porter argues that most companies remain stuck in a "social responsibility" mindset in which societal issues are at the periphery, not the core. Instead, companies can benefit by creating shared value, by reconceiving products and markets, redefining productivity in the value chain, and enabling local cluster development. This leads businesses to discover new approaches that generate greater innovation and growth – and also benefits for society. Corporations have the opportunity to use their skills, resources and management capability to lead social progress in ways that even the best-intentioned government and social sector organisations can rarely match. In doing this, business can regain the trust and respect of society.[30]

30 Michael E Porter and Mark R. Kramer (2011) Creating shared value: how to reinvent capitalism – and unleash a wave of innovation and growth, *Harvard Business Review*, January-February 2011

Organisations can evolve through five main stages of maturity, with each stage offering greater potential for creating real business value and sustainable outcomes. In the first stage, the concern is primarily for legal compliance – doing the minimum required by law and no more. The second stage includes but transcends the first; greater focus is applied to identifying and managing business risks. The third stage includes a concern for efficient use of resources, both to minimise business costs and to demonstrate responsible resource stewardship. Evolution to the fourth stage involves a growing concern for socially responsible business practices and community development. The fifth stage sees the emergence of an organisation that is regarded as a strategic, innovative leader – changing the game for business and developing new business models that create shared value through new, more sustainable and profitable assets, products and services.

Where is your organisation now?

Business value

compliance

risk managem⁺

eco-efficiency

corporate responsibility

leadership and innovation

maturity of their approach

Yet creating "shared value" remains an idea and aspiration for the vast majority of organisations. Recent surveys have revealed most organisations fall into the "risk management" and "eco-efficiency" categories on the maturity spectrum – IBM reported that only 8 per cent of surveyed organisations across 26 industries and 31 countries were regarded as true innovators (most of which were in the consumer products sectors) – seeing sustainability as a growth driver and core business differentiator rather than a corporate social responsibility (CSR) and cost efficiency driver.[31]

The most progressive and innovative organisations look at sustainability differently – both in terms of business opportunity and in the way in which they operate. While aggressively pursuing growth they are also more likely to invest in communities, crowd-source for innovation, and collaborate with other industry stakeholders. GE stands out in this field with its Ecomagination division, which develops technologies enabling everything from smart grid optimisation to water conservation, nanofiltration, portable desalination and high-efficiency engine operation.[32] As a business strategy, Ecomagination has been a great success. The Ecomagination portfolio includes more than 140 products and solutions, and has generated more than US$105 billion in revenue to 2011, exceeding business growth targets and growing at a faster rate than the rest of GE.

So business leaders are well served to recognise that responses to sustainability can fall within a wide spectrum, from mere compliance activities to major decisions about capital allocation for growth, market entry and exit strategies, and which capabilities to acquire via mergers and acquisitions. These are, of course, far from trivial decisions.

31 IBM Institute for Business Value (2011) *Driving performance through sustainability – strategy, synergy and significance*, IBM Global Services, New York

32 http://files.gecompany.com/ecomagination/progress/GE_ecomagination_2011AnnualReport.pdf

Set goals

While it might seem obvious to set goals, the importance of this task is often misunderstood. If done well, it's a valuable process because goals signal what matters and convey performance expectations. In effect, the goal-setting dialogue responds to the question *What level of performance is required and by when to achieve acceptable business improvement?* and is the vehicle through which "buy-in" can be tested and confirmed.

Furthermore, goals provide a benchmark against which to plan execution tactics, to evaluate the implementation cost (particularly in the absence of methods to ascribe a value to externalities), to review performance, and to discuss and agree upon improvement actions.

Take the example

Our firm set a target to reduce greenhouse gas emissions by 30 per cent per staff member over 3 years without resorting to carbon offsets. Firstly we had to understand the source of our emissions, and then determine the most cost-effective means to cut them. It transpired that the major sources of emissions included building tenancies (that is, electricity use) and air, rail and road travel. Reducing building emissions, while not without its challenges, was more straightforward than cutting travel emissions, particularly when this involved the collective decisions of several hundred people involved in client-related and internal corporate travel in any one week. Emissions data was regularly collected, transcribed from paper invoices to a database, analysed and reported to inform decisions about ongoing improvement. Over time, a number of internal business systems were improved and the data collection automated, which also helped identify errors in our accounts and incorrect bills from suppliers to the firm, leading to cost savings. With ongoing coordinated effort based on good information, we reduced the firm's emissions by over 35 per cent in 3 years, simultaneously reducing our annual operating costs by well over US$300,000. Today we apply an internal price on carbon of US$15 per tonne to each of our operations centres, raising several hundred thousand dollars to invest in further emissions reduction. Our firm is also more aware of client carbon emissions, noting that proactive effort on our part to reduce emissions in the large industrial operations of our clients could effectively offset our remaining emissions. All this occurred because of a single target that we set.

Providing structure and translation

We have found it useful to provide a basic structure that links an organisation's material issues, sustainability goals and business maturity. This helps translate and communicate the connection between sustainability, core business and competitive strategies.

The structure can get people thinking about the current maturity of core business competencies, and where improvement in those competencies can enhance the sustainability of the organisation and deliver greater value to shareholders and stakeholders – importantly, articulated in the language of the audience.

Such a framework can also help people in the organisation to see what's involved, why it's important and who's responsible for implementing aspects of the sustainability strategy. Importantly, it will show clear initiatives that comprise a program that's much more than reducing waste or environmental impact. It translates sustainability beyond a green agenda and confusing, vague jargon into clear and concrete initiatives articulated in the language of day-to-day business in an integrated way.

The five-stage model of business sustainability and maturity can be developed to provide a road map for business improvement tactics. It can help focus on practical, complementary actions to drive business improvement, highlighting and filling capability, process or performance gaps where they exist while keeping an eye on the end game. It also provides a useful framework for benchmarking performance within or between organisations.

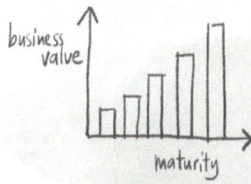

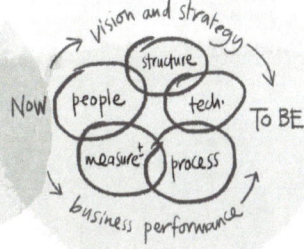

Business improvement tactics road map

business value

maturity

Now

vision and strategy
people
structure
tech.
measure+
process
business performance
TO BE

Org. competencies	five stage model					where we are now	how we bridge the gap	where we want to be	goals and targets
	COMPLIANCE	RISK MANAGEMENT	ECO EFFICIENCY	CORP. RESPONSIBILITY	LEADERSHIP & INNOV.				
Why leadership									
What strategies customer focus goods/products services									
How people culture capabilities governance management									

Take the example Sustainable outcomes were a priority for a large and complex liquid natural gas project. The project owner had defined corporate sustainability values because it felt that the delivery of good social and environmental outcomes was crucial to its business success. Yet there was no mechanism, process or tool to incorporate them in the gas project.

A "sustainability roadmap" was developed with the project team, discussing the sustainability values and prioritising them against each of the major design tasks. The design tasks rated as high priority design were those with a high potential to affect the value or outcome – for better or worse. This was structured as a matrix that mapped the 20 project tasks against the 36 sustainability outcomes the project and its owner needed to achieve. The project manager reflected, "*This is what really made the difference. The team was looking for structure and a logical roadmap to follow that easily identified the priority issues to consider in the design from the outset. We now had a tool to do this.*"

The project's sustainability manager subsequently developed a set of practical design guidelines for each of the 36 outcomes. This provided simple but practical advice to any team member at any stage of the project – advice on how to apply sustainable design principles to their task. "*We haven't seen anything like this before – it made sustainability real. And it's just what we needed as practical prompts for what to consider when we are doing sustainable design.*" Importantly, the project team was involved in its development, so the tool was relevant and practical, and there was senior task-leader support. It was highly effective, and resulted in the team reframing project problems in ways that saved time and money and also avoided community complaints.

Executing strategy involves change

Having addressed "why" sustainability is relevant to core business, it's important to expose "how" the business goals will be achieved.

A good business strategy aims to enhance organisational performance – either in terms of the magnitude and effectiveness of service delivery for public enterprises, or by creating a point of positive differentiation and competitive advantage in the goods, services and products provided by private enterprise. Invariably this means making changes in the business – refinements or more substantial transformations and business initiatives. So almost by definition, implementing strategy involves making and managing change.

This aspect of business leadership and improvement is often poorly appreciated, particularly the time and measures required to effectively execute change, and this is a key factor explaining the failure of many business improvement initiatives.

Decades of management research has consistently shown that two-thirds of strategies and change management efforts fail to deliver the anticipated results because of defects and breakdowns in planning and execution. And why is this? Because organisations often do not take the holistic approach required to see the change through.

Arguments can rage over whether the failure is due to poor people or bad process. Yet no company plans to hire bad people, and indeed most people want to do a good job. So process is important. Indeed, the majority of companies in the top quartile of financial performance combine attention to strategy execution process with attention to developing their people.[33]

Equally, leading change does not imply that senior managers are, or should be, "all knowing" while the rest of the organisation are arms and legs that merely carry out management's bidding.[34] Such an approach damages an organisation because it alienates the people working for it. Instead, when people's choices are valued and feedback is encouraged, employees send information upward, improving the knowledge base of decision makers higher up and helping everyone in the organisation do better.

While many frameworks exist to help plan and guide organisational change management (like those offered by John Kotter and McKinsey & Co.), the core ideas are very similar and in essence build upon the common observation that multiple complementary measures are required to effectively execute change.

Neither a change in structure nor in people's performance goals alone will deliver the desired results. Only by pulling multiple "levers" in sequence will the conditions and capabilities be created to enable and motivate people to change their decisions and behaviours in line with organisational strategy.

Furthermore, these multiple levers are likely to be within the control of a range of functional teams within organisations, and thus alignment with strategy is essential to effectively execute change.

So being able to lead change is a core business competency for a modern sustainable enterprise – a view strongly endorsed by a majority of global CEOs canvassed by IBM in 2010. It found that the top-performing organisations that surpass their industry peers in terms of revenue growth and profitability place an emphasis on openness, collaboration and change management capabilities. Compared with underperformers, 73 per cent more out-performers excel at managing change.[35]

33 http://knowledge.wharton.upenn.edu/article.cfm?articleid=1252

34 http://hbr.org/2010/07/the-execution-trap/ar/1?conversationId=60167

35 IBM (2010) *Capitalising on complexity: insights from the global CEO study*, IBM Institute for Business Value, New York

Strategic development and business growth – from a current "as is" state to a future designed "to be" state – involves change. Successfully managing that change so the desired strategy sticks requires a range of complementary measures to be implemented simultaneously. Failure to recognise this requirement, or to effectively design and execute complementary measures, is a key reason why so many organisational change initiatives fail. Leadership and alignment of people and resources is critical to creating the culture and behaviours that make change possible.

(Adapted from Jay R Gailbraith, *Designing Organisations*, 1995)

Organisational design

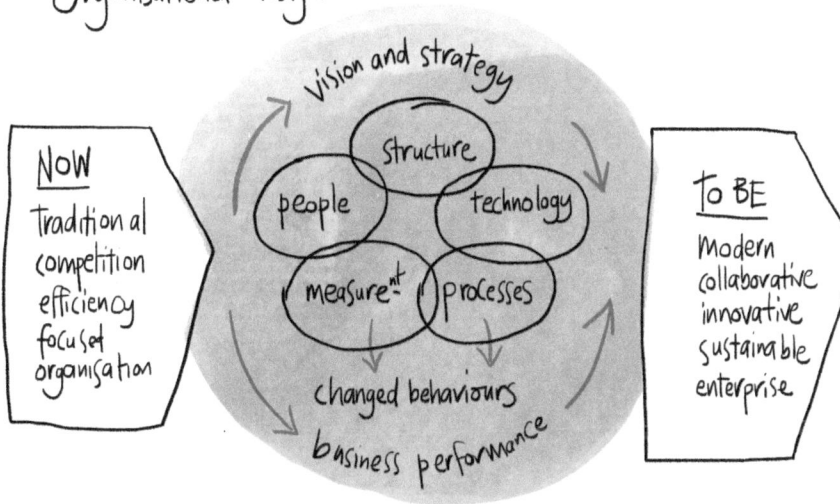

NOW
Traditional
competition
efficiency
focused
organisation

Vision and strategy
Structure
people
technology
measure^t
processes
changed behaviours
business performance

To BE
Modern
collaborative
innovative
sustainable
enterprise

Problem solve with implementers

Just as sustainability issues and opportunities can elude management teams, it can also be a vague concept to people at the coalface. Staff may perceive sustainability as a set of environmental issues relevant to only one department, a green PR agenda, or worse, as spin. To ensure people understand the business objectives, and buy into them, engage them with the translated framework and goals, and in the process of problem solving ways to meet those goals.

When engaging different teams within an organisation, it's important to recognise that different divisions of a business can contribute to the same goals.

Take the example A water utility working to translate its sustainability objectives into executable plans involved each of its business groups, including finance, customer relations and water supply operations. Each group was charged with developing relevant and connected improvement tactics that helped deliver on the utility's stated community, environmental and financial goals. While the contributions different business groups can make vary significantly, people nonetheless know where they fit in and the role they play in achieving sustainable outcomes for their businesses and communities. Sustainability and smart business have become one, not separate issues. A senior operations manager commented: *"Can you believe that I now have truck drivers arguing for smarter maintenance solutions that they are describing in financial, environmental and community terms? When they get out of the truck now, they're not only thinking "safety first" but also about sustainable solutions."*

So this process supports stronger engagement with the people who need to implement sustainability initiatives. It also allows customisation of those initiatives for the respective business groups.

Engage the resource managers

When the Board and executive team have developed and signed off on the corporate strategy it is only a document and "espoused strategy". What actually gets done on the ground – the real investments made and actions taken – determine what strategy is really implemented. So the people who control the allocation of time, effort and resources each day are pivotal to determining what gets done. Typically this means we are talking about "middle management" and controllers of business processes.

However, they can often resist change because they don't have sufficient input in shaping those initiatives. Too often, they lack the tools, the language, and the forums in which to express legitimate concerns about the design and implementation of change projects.[36]

So again, it's critically important to involve this group of people in planning and executing the required initiatives, where appropriate facilitating a dialogue with senior executives to ensure messages and expectations are clear and consistent.

36 http://hbr.org/2005/10/the-hard-side-of-change-management/ar/1

Private sector companies surveyed by MIT Sloan Management Review[37] indicate 57 per cent of businesses expect employee interest in sustainability to affect their organisations.

Over one-third of companies (37 per cent) already highlight sustainability initiatives in recruiting and around 43 per cent are drawing on employees to be part of the process by designing products or processes for reuse or recycling.

Work with the willing

While it's necessary and appropriate to work with people in formal, line management roles to drive change, one must not forget that leaders exist at many levels in different roles.

"People are hungry for the opportunity to work professionally in a way that is consistent with building a sustainable world instead of one that undermines it," says John Sterman, a professor at America's MIT Sloan School of Management and director of MIT's System Dynamics Group. "The idea that 'I'm going to work in a corporation that may have the impact of further degrading the capacity of the planet to support life and then in my spare time I'm going to use the money that I've made to do good deeds' — that just doesn't cut it for people anymore. You can't have that kind of dissonance."

This willingness of people to seek out activities that contribute to more than a project itself, and its powerful and often unexpected benefits were evident when our company was working on a project to build new retail outlets for a major oil company in India. Our staff working onsite spent their lunch hours teaching English to the local construction workforce and our firm subsequently invested in this activity through its corporate community investment scheme. This additional effort and commitment was so valued by the Indian construction crews that they chose to move around the country to new sites with us, saving time and effort recruiting new local construction teams and generating substantial benefits in productivity and safe work practices.

37 http://sloanreview.mit.edu/the-magazine/2009-fall/51110/does-sustainability-change-the-talent-equation/

Take the example

One person can change a business model – and redefine value

The company we work with wanted to engage a commercial cleaner for a major new office block, which was aiming for a recognised sustainability rating. Four companies were invited to tender.

The administration officer overseeing the process wondered if it didn't offer a chance to "put sustainability into practice". She added sustainability criteria to the tender inviting companies to detail approaches for a more sustainable performance of their products and equipment.

The response was interesting. Three of the companies didn't respond at all to these criteria, with no suggestions or information provided except for the basics on price. The fourth company was quite different. It put forward a range of solutions to reduce its chemical and water use and to minimise maintenance and reduce waste and toxic waste. It also requested a longer contract to provide the financial security to invest in new techniques and equipment to achieve these benefits. We agreed, and the company won the job. We later heard that this innovative approach and sustainability credentials set this company up to consistently win contracts against its competitors.

Interestingly, the three unsuccessful companies in the tender contacted us a few months later to advise they had got organised, had launched some good sustainability initiatives and would be interested in tendering in future.

A single person at a small scale who asked one simple but good question successfully changed the attitudes and performance of not just one, but four major cleaning businesses servicing most of the city. Just think what a similar approach could initiate across larger procurement contracts.

Leadership matters

It should be very clear by now that enabling high-value, transformative change in favour of business and society is very achievable but does require deliberate, thoughtful and sustained attention. Unsurprisingly, *leadership matters*. We find the leaders of many organisations will sincerely aspire to, and work diligently for, significant improvement in their organisation and its performance, yet on any objective assessment they would best be described as managers, not leaders.

Leaders create change, while managers seek stability and efficiency.

Developing and implementing any worthwhile organisational strategy takes time, as does its execution. So to be worthwhile and effective, the tactics need to be targeted to deliver the right outcomes at some future point in time. That is, good strategy responds to emerging (not current) needs. It follows that middle managers (resource allocators and determinants of what strategy is actually executed) and staff are unlikely to experience "pain" or crisis in the current moment to motivate their action in favour of the future-focused strategy. Thus, leadership is again paramount if strategy is to be implemented "ahead of the curve".

So this makes the task of leading the change one for a senior executive. What are the characteristics of effective leaders in the sustainability space? The next chapter explores this question further, drawing on first-hand experience.

USEFUL QUESTIONS

- **How do you know the business leaders are committed to pursuing sustainable development?**

- **What are the actions that matter most to improving the business or project outcomes?**

- **Do you have a structured plan to lead change that involves the people who will implement it "on the ground"?**

Eleven

It's about leading change

Sustainability leaders are not environmental zealots – they are accomplished business leaders, integrators and entrepreneurs.

Technical skills are important, but not as important as communication skills.

Simple, practical language and action is vital.

"The first responsibility of a
leader is to define reality."

Max De Pree, former CEO of Herman Miller, Inc.[38]

38   In *Leadership is an Art*, Dell Publishing, 1989

Take the example A regional utility based in the Asia-Pacific had an energetic sustainability manager who was largely ineffective. She focused on the small, internal matters such as office supplies, tended to "lecture" and failed to connect to the wider business. Her focus was on the peripheral activities that were easy to resolve, and not the hard, complex challenge of how to influence the organisation's core strategies and priorities. Our assessment was that she lacked the level of experience and influencing skills to see the strategic connections and navigate her way effectively through this maze, and so adopted a lower-risk (and lower-impact) approach. The way her role was set up by the organisation to have a strong operational rather than strategic focus positioned it from the start to be ineffective.

She left, and the organisation then worked with our sustainability team, who identified the real need and focused their effort on demonstrating the relevance of sustainability to the business. The result? Sustainability is now embedded across the whole organisation, drives strategy and investments, and has changed its culture. The essential difference was one of "soft" skills and strategic thinking, not just technical smarts.

So the Board has just adopted a Sustainability Policy for your organisation, and you as the Sustainability Manager now have the role of "making it happen".

Congratulations! What do you do now? Where do you start?

You will need to go well beyond policy. Having a sustainability policy will be an important signal of your organisation's intent and commitment. But once developed, the policy is the start, and not the end. Your role is how to execute it; to operationalise into the business; to make it relevant and central to all the organisation's core activities. You will need to do this at a scale beyond those who are interested and supportive. This means avoiding the easy path, which is to confine your activities and sphere of influence to just "working with the willing". This can be a useful starting point, but you will need to move beyond this zone of comfort and easy wins.

Interestingly, the last areas to focus on are technical information and factual detail. The essence of your task is to engage, challenge and motivate, to change attitudes and behaviours that may have been set for decades, and essentially to effect change across the organisation. You may have come from a strong technical or operations management background with high credibility in your discipline, but you are about to enter the world of the change agent. It's more nebulous and uncertain, but the rewards are immense.

Most likely this will challenge you in a way no previous role has, and will require you to develop new skills. The challenge – and opportunity – for you is that these skills will be "soft skills" – influencing, communication and facilitation coupled with strategy development. Without mastering these, you are unlikely to be effective.

Who are the sustainability leaders?

Sustainability leadership roles began emerging in the early 2000s and now present a professional career path, particularly in larger organisations, although in some geographies senior executive leadership positions are still relatively uncommon. For example, by mid-2011 only 29 companies among the roughly 7,000 publicly-traded companies (listed on the NYSE or NASDAQ) in the United States had instituted Chief Sustainability Officers (CSO).[39] Outside the USA, roughly a third of organisations identified as having CSOs reporting directly to the CEO.

Does your organisation need an executive-level position to lead sustainability initiatives? In all likelihood, if you are serious about embracing the insights in this book and dealing with the risks and opportunities that fall under the banner of sustainability, the answer is "yes".

We believe this to be the case for a few reasons. It's not that people in other roles, like a head of strategy, innovation or possibly HSEC (health, safety, environment and community), could not theoretically take on the responsibility. But these people will already have busy roles and are unlikely to have the capacity to absorb the volume of new knowledge that comes with this territory, and the ability to put it to effect. Further, their strong competencies may not be well aligned; the most effective CSOs also tend to have a unique combination of skills that are less likely to be exhibited in people leading functions that are well understood, defined and structured. It's also important to recognise that there is no necessary correlation between a CSO and environmental professionals such as environmental scientists or engineers. Such an appointment could reinforce a view that "sustainability = environment" if the person doesn't drive the more strategic agenda that's required.

Finally, the appointment of a CSO provides a very clear and visible signal to internal and external stakeholders that your organisation is taking sustainability seriously – something likely to be received as a positive by investors, insurers and staff.

39 Weinreb Group (2011) *CSO back story: how Chief Sustainability Officers reached the C-Suite*, September 2011. http://weinrebgroup.com/wp-content/uploads/2011/09/CSO-Back-Story-by-Weinreb-Group.pdf

The nature of CSOs

Several studies have researched the types of people filling the new roles of a Chief Sustainability Officer (CSO). In brief, they possess skills in leading business transformation, general management and innovation – different from a typical business leader for risk, health and safety, or corporate philanthropy. They are typically systems thinkers, good networkers who can connect cross-functional teams and have an eye for strategy, translating external factors into internal opportunities. They do not define themselves as environmentalists and often have diverse academic qualifications, ranging from a bachelor's degree to a PhD in business management, public policy or science.

Furthermore, CSOs tend to be business veterans who have worked their way up through the ranks, often having held an external-facing role, so they understand more intimately the core business of servicing customers; those surveyed by Verdantix had been employed with their company for an average of 16 years before taking on the role of CSO.

CSOs in progressive global businesses like Unilever and IKEA are generally in charge of large and growing budgets (but not necessarily their own P&L), and are responsible for massive strategic transformation programs. And despite the global financial crisis, 85 per cent of 250 CSO budgets around the world are reported to be maintained or growing.[40] Yet CSOs don't often have a large number of direct reports (often five or less). Instead they manage nimble operations with few resources but a growing, often company-wide team supporting their efforts.

40 Verdantix (2012) Global Sustainability Leaders Survey: Budgets and Priorities, Verdantix Ltd, London

More than an operational role

While sustainability leadership roles have
evolved over the past decade, some remain
rooted in compliance and risk management
functions. Although the related issues are clearly
important, it is really managing a "business as
usual" approach.

We are also seeing the sustainability manager
role emerging on major projects delivered
through formal alliances or joint ventures which
involve large teams over an extended period.
As they establish their own organisation and
culture, the same skills apply to the role in this
context.

Sustainability isn't like safety

Don't for a minute let people suggest your role
is similar to that of introducing a safety program
within an organisation. Safety has strong
and well-entrenched legislative drivers and a
"burning platform" with business directors and
managers subject to criminal charges arising
from safety incidents. Safety also has immediate
and direct connections to our personal
wellbeing and self-interest, and it is very
tangible and visible. We all understand what
safety means and almost universally agree that
it's a good thing to do; sustainability is often a
confused term and can generate strong positive
and negative reactions. Added to this are the
benefits from decades of safety data collection
to develop well-substantiated, quantifiable
cases. Sustainability has few of these attributes,
which suggests why the role of a sustainability
leader is that much more challenging.

So where do you start?

There is no recipe or guide book for this role, and few well-documented examples of an effective process. What follows are a few insights and suggestions, based very much on lessons learnt and the wisdom of hindsight.

Focus on the big stuff. The successful sustainability managers we see know how to make the most impact in their organisation and know where the critical points of decision making are. Resolving the multitude of internal issues such as purchasing recycled paper, turning off computer screens or purchasing fair trade coffee is relevant and valued highly by some staff – but it will consume you, and more than likely result in minimal impact compared with the opportunities in other areas of your business. Let others tackle these issues, and instead focus on how you can influence the main activities and impacts of your organisation. Be open and honest, and don't apologise about where you're putting your effort and why.

Translate sustainability into meaningful terms. An essential attribute of this role is the ability to translate and demonstrate the relevance of sustainability to the organisation and its business. This is not just about mega-trends and global issues; it is also your organisation's strategic priorities and how these are implemented. Making the connection between the sustainability agenda, corporate needs and existing business processes is fundamental if you are to be effective. Weak translation of sustainability into simple, practical language and actions that are meaningful to staff and reflect the organisation's culture and activities is a recipe for being marginalised.

Take the example

Gaining interest, support and action for sustainability from senior influencers in our organisation (7,000 staff across several continents) was a major task and required careful planning and execution. A series of 1-day workshops were designed to demonstrate the power of the strategic thinking tools and processes we had developed for use across the firm's projects for more sustainable outcomes. The workshop was very hands-on and centred around the challenges of a real prospect or project of the firm to which participants could apply their technical expertise to solve. We also carefully selected workshop participants to ensure a senior and diverse group. Innovative solutions with significant practical value were always developed. This was exciting, inspiring and empowering, and showed a real contribution from staff to an issue that was relevant to our business and a process that could make a real difference.

It's just a fad and the latest buzzword

I CAN'T SEE HOW IT'S RELEVANT TO THIS PROJECT

THIS LOOKS GOOD ... AS LONG AS IT DOESN'T COST MORE

this will inspire me

Connect with people on their level. People in your organisation will be at different points of the "sustainability readiness" spectrum and you can't ignore that. You must hear what they have to say and respond thoughtfully if your approach is to be successful. Understand the hidden assumptions and underlying beliefs that are held by many staff. Get them out on the table as the basis for a robust and honest discussion. Common attitudes we've experienced include: *"Sustainability adds cost and will complicate projects"*, *"It's a greenie issue"*, *"We're already doing it!"* and *"It's just a fad. I'm sick of the word and it turns me off."* Unless you expose these views to discussion, they can continue to influence attitudes and behaviours in negative ways. Telling staff they are wrong won't help – the persuasion comes from examples, stories, and evidence from recent projects.

And just as we've outlined before, use questions to stimulate discussion, particularly between peers with different levels of appreciation of sustainability. They can effectively influence each other and help develop understanding – you don't need to answer every question! Indeed, it's useful to recognise that engineers and scientists relish a good problem to solve. A "telling" or " teaching" approach would fail miserably. Framing the issues as problems that require their expertise to solve is both engaging and demonstrates relevance to their work, rather than imposing an additional task.

Read, read and read. Take advantage of the books, websites and other information available about successful organisational and behavioural change and keep ahead with your knowledge. A good understanding of effective approaches and innovations that others are trying is useful. Your previous technical expertise won't be the ingredient that makes you effective and successful in this role. Becoming familiar with these change principles and how to facilitate them is essential.

Take the example In an effort to influence our approach to infrastructure design, we asked: "Where are the best opportunities to reduce our energy use and greenhouse gas emissions across the whole process?" The reply was: ***"We don't really know – no one has really looked at the total process in this way before."*** That single question resulted in a major piece of research working closely with the client, two conference papers at international conferences, liaison with universities and researchers across Australia, interest from other utilities internationally, and importantly, a better and more energy efficient design.

our clients don't want it. Really?

"Sustainability is not relevant to us. Our clients just don't want it," commented a colleague. "Really?" we replied, "So when you say they don't want 'it', what does 'it' mean?" This was a great start to dialogue on what sustainability means to our clients, and the perceptions and barriers that existed to pursuing more sustainable solutions. The question goes straight to the heart of the challenge for many sustainability professionals. "Sustainability" is seen by some as an over-used label that closes thinking and opportunities.

"Are you saying our clients don't want to lessen their risks, lower whole-of-life costs, or gain a stronger social licence to operate? What about reduced project approvals times, or project designs that are more resilient and adaptable over time?" This language triggered a more meaningful and receptive discussion. We actually developed a popular resource: "20 great questions to ask around sustainability without using the 's' word".

making it real and practical

- - - - - - - - - - - - -
To make
sustainability
accessible to all
staff, we developed
communication tools
containing:

– the 5 questions you
  should ask on every
  project

– the 7 steps to apply
  sustainability in every
  project;

– the 6 sustainable
  outcomes you should
  strive for on every
  project.

This conveyed the
essentials about
sustainability in a way
that was practical and
accessible to all. It also
kept the message alive.
- - - - - - - - - - - - - - - - -

The next steps

Enlist pragmatic influencers. There may be many people in your organisation with a passion for sustainability and zeal to "convert" others. Despite the best of intentions, the zealot will alienate your staff, be impervious to their perspectives, and fail to influence constructively. This is not to say that you won't need supporters at all levels in the organisation, particularly in middle management. It's just that they need to be similarly skilled – at sound business leadership and influencing, with a basis for credibility. These champions will quickly emerge, sometimes from the most unexpected quarters.

Be persistent. You will also need plenty of persistence and resilience. In the absence of a crisis or a burning, urgent platform for action, many people will be uninterested, or actively resist the need for change. Another key factor at play here is inertia. While the logic and reasons to incorporate sustainability into work practices may resonate with many, the forces that maintain the status quo and keep people doing what they have always done run deep.

Always keep it practical, relevant and simple. Sustainability typically is perceived as complex and nebulous. Thoughtful simplicity should be your aim. This is not dumbing down, but distilling the essentials – really critical elements that are relevant to your organisation.

Take the example

Few team members of a project we were working on felt they understood sustainability – many felt it was jargon, a "greenie fad" of little relevance to the project. Two Board members from a construction manager background had such attitudes. Out of politeness (and probably curiosity), they requested a meeting to try and understand what it all meant. We prepared assiduously, and went armed with many hard-hitting practical examples of sustainable outcomes with specific dollar benefits. Our conversation was going quite well, but took a surprising turn when they starting asking about vision and the long-term future legacy. This was what got them excited – a project legacy that in a small way made the world a better place. We had a great discussion, and they left as inspired and strong advocates for the sustainability program who used their influence on the Board to build further support. We still remember their parting words: *"This has been inspiring. And we thought sustainability was for hippies in tie-dyed T-shirts and sandals!"*

How do you demonstrate achievement?

One real challenge is to demonstrate progress and achievements. As with any change program, the outcomes can be indirect, occur over a period of time or be masked by a range of other influencing factors. Meaningful metrics of success can be difficult to develop. So what will success look like – in tangible terms? How will you demonstrate the impact you and the sustainability program are having? It's worth thinking early on how you will do this, so measurement and reporting can be designed as part of management activities from the start.

Take the example We used a mix of hard statistics, powerful stories, quotes, anecdotes and case studies to illustrate the achievements and impact of our sustainability program. A staff awareness and engagement program had detailed information showing its global reach and levels of participation. This was supplemented by follow-up surveys of all staff to demonstrate the impact of the program on behaviours one and three months down the track. It was the most rigorous evaluation program ever undertaken by the company on an internal program, and built real confidence the sustainability team was implementing a robust, well-executed approach. It also gave useful information that helped shape the way the program evolved, and gave transferable insights that continue to benefit other business programs.

Communicate, communicate, communicate

This is a simple but important message that many recognised business leaders would agree with. It's easy to get consumed in tasks and details, and lose connection with the people you are seeking to influence. Keep your message alive, demonstrating connection to people in their various roles, talking about successes and progress, and keeping people motivated all take time. Face-to-face communication is also most powerful, particularly when you can tell stories that reflect the change you are trying to bring about. So we'll say it again – communicate often.

A sustainability leader is not a sustainability zealot, but a strategic influencer of people, and connector of ideas and resources. Their IQ is matched by their EQ (emotional intelligence) and personal resilience to progressively influence people and drive changes in mindsets and behaviours.

USEFUL QUESTIONS

- **How do you know you have the right person in the sustainability leadership role?**

- **Can you describe, in less than 30 seconds, the purpose of your sustainability agenda and the key things you are trying to achieve?**

- **How can you present sustainability in a way that is practical, relevant and compelling to different audiences, including the Board, management and staff?**

Twelve

Rules for sustainability tools

Decide what you want a sustainability tool to achieve.

Simple is always best.

Present results in the most powerful way.

"A tool is but the extension
of a man's hand."

Henry Ward Beecher,
American social reformer, 1887

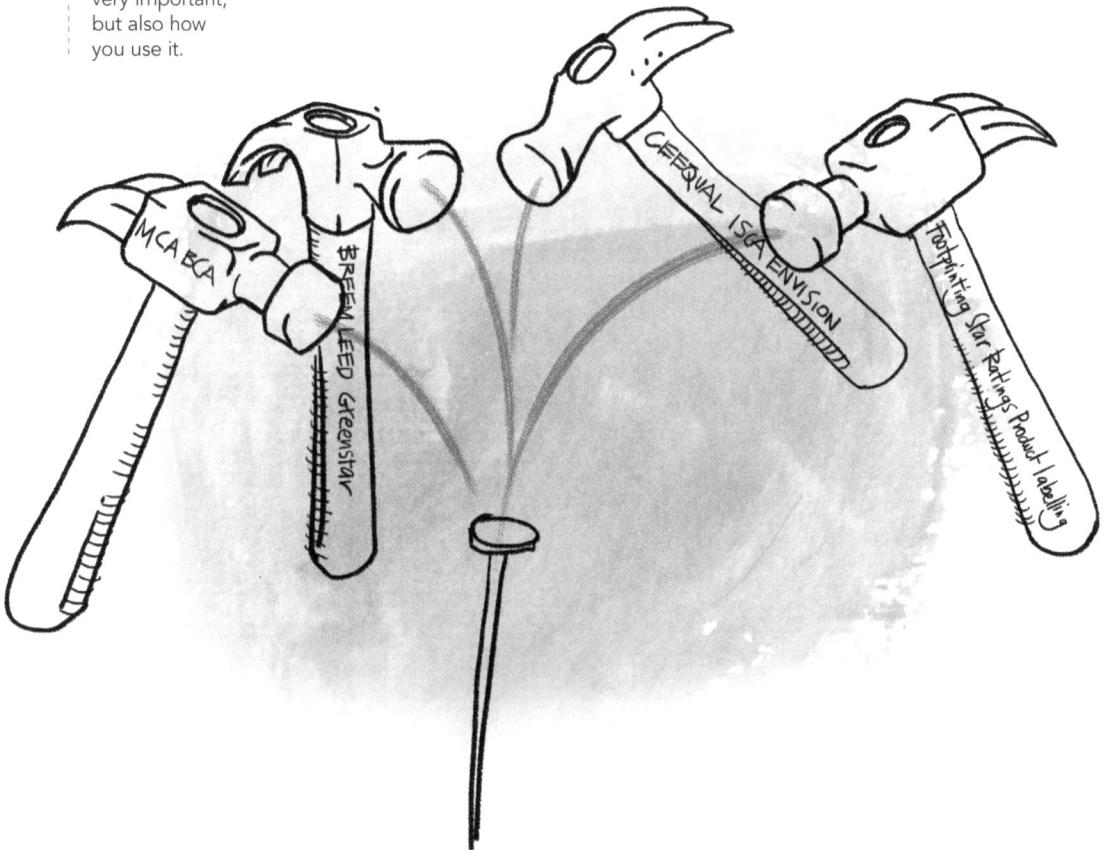

"If all you have is a hammer,
everything looks like a nail"

Bernard Baruch
American investor, philanthropist and
Presidential advisor

Not only is the
choice of tool
very important,
but also how
you use it.

Take the example

This was clear in the experience of a team we worked with that was charged with finding the "best" location for a major regional aerodrome. It required assessment of many complex and sometimes competing elements. The local council needed a transparent assessment framework to demonstrate it had selected the most sustainable site – that is, the location that delivered the greatest long-term benefits for residents, businesses, passengers, aircraft operators and the environment, while also achieving a solid economic return on investment.

When we first started, the client had a much narrower view and believed what mattered was cost, noise, compatibility with future urban expansion and safety. Our team had various expertise, including an economist specialising in air infrastructure as well as social, environmental and urban planners. This was important in bringing a broader perspective to the key factors in selecting the "best" location. Additional factors quickly emerged, including the need to support local business development, bushfire risk, stormwater flooding, connectivity with other transport modes, and the impact on valuable open space. Ensuring a viable role into the future given other planned aerodrome expansions in the region was also important.

We initially developed a long list of 43 possible criteria to assess the location options, built by progressively adding criteria as the issues were identified. The economist on the work team finally said, "*There are just too many criteria that really assess the same thing, but are just expressed in different ways. It's double counting.*"

We worked through each criterion to identify what each was really assessing, which quickly revealed duplication. The 43 criteria were eventually refined to just 18. Our project team and client found this process important. As one team member said: "*It has helped us draw out the attributes that really matter. The process has made us clarify our thinking, and we feel we have got to the core of the most important factors that influence location.*"

A preferred option emerged from the tool's application, and was accepted by the Council. As the senior project manager put it: "*I'm happy to support the recommended option as I am confident in the outcome and how to we got to it.*" This experience reminded us that a tool with a robust and inclusive process that has a clear logic and comprehensive structure gives confidence in the outcome.

What is a sustainability tool?

Where do you start with sustainability tools and frameworks? What exactly are they, and what can they achieve? How do you find the best tools, and will they actually add value?

Tools are the means to an end, not an end in themselves. The end objective is to influence good decisions. So having a clear understanding about the nature and scope of that decision, who is involved in making it and how best to influence them, will shape the way you select the most appropriate tool as well as the process for applying it and communicating the outcome. The people aspect of sustainability tools can be easily overlooked, but tools don't make decisions – people do.

We generally define a sustainability "tool" as a framework or methodology that scopes, structures, assesses and demonstrates the key attributes for the most sustainable outcome. They provide a structure and logic to work through complex and often connected issues, allow an informed comparison of alternatives and help with developing or selecting the "best" strategy or design option. Effective sustainability tools apply a broad lens to the problem, which avoids a narrow perspective that flows through to the assessment.

There's a plethora of sustainability tools available today (20 million references on Google and growing) and they employ different methodologies as well as various weightings, levels of quantification and rating to achieve different objectives. Tools can be seen along a spectrum. At one end are those with tightly defined methodologies and highly quantified and specific outputs that are typically ratified by industry bodies and even governments. Carbon footprinting and life cycle assessments are examples. At the other end are tools for scoping high-level strategic alternatives, priorities and direction.

Tools can offer a *process* for strategic, innovative thinking. The "Sustainability by Design" toolkit we've developed for use across projects with clients does just that. It provides a structured and facilitated process to foster collaborative, integrated approaches that challenge professionals to understand the wider context of their project, and to see it part of a connected system. Somewhere in between are those tools that assess various project or design options.

Whatever the challenge, you'll find a relevant tool or framework that allows you to deliver a more sustainable outcome. The challenge is deciding *what you want the tool to achieve*. It's helpful to start with the end in mind. What is your end objective?

For tools to be most effective they should assist in three ways:

- provide a structure that brings clarity and logic to fully understanding the problem and the material issues,

- apply a process that involves and builds the understanding of relevant others,

- clearly differentiates the preferred option and demonstrate its benefits.

All tools are designed by someone, and the designer brings (even unconsciously) their own perspectives, preferences and worldview to the tool's construction. Beware the subtle bias. As an example, some frameworks can have a marked focus on factors that can be more readily quantified (volume of materials, water and power use, carbon emissions), while social and community factors are descriptive and lack rigour.

Based on our experience of various sustainability tools and frameworks as well as the insights we gained from developing our own tool, we've compiled a set of *Rules for Sustainability Tools*. These can be applied to any sustainability tool or framework when assessing its relevance and worth to your organisation or project.

Rule 1 – A logical structure is everything

Why? Because an effective structure organises information, issues and outcomes in a way that "makes sense" of complexity, and draws focus to the most material issues. It needs to develop a logic that flows through the assessment to fully understand the real problem and its causal factors. A complex tool with excessive detail will fail to provide clarity and confidence in the outcomes. Being comprehensive is not the same as including everything. A solid structure and good process is logical and repeatable, and can be fine-tuned or tailored for applications across a range of decisions. It also provides a transparent audit trail.

Take the example — The importance of a logical structure in a sustainability tool came home to us when developing a "sustainability and investment scorecard" for a government Water Trust with a budget in the hundreds of millions for worthwhile water projects. The problem was that no money had been invested for over a year, at a time of severe drought that was affecting cities and regional communities. It seemed the Trust lacked confidence to judge and select projects to invest in; these could come to them as proposals at any time. Executives were frustrated and wanted a sound decision support tool. "We are bright people – why is this so hard?" they said. Yet their resolve was strong. "We have to make progress on this, and we just need a framework to work within to make robust decisions."

Through discussions it became clear they were expecting a multi-criteria analysis tool in the form of a spreadsheet. What they got was something different – and more effective – to the extent that the Chairman of the Trust said: "We asked for an apple and you gave us an orange…but it's a terrific orange!"

So what happened? We starting by looking at the business scope, purpose and the decisions that were needed, and heard the needs and frustrations of staff. It seemed there was one key barrier to progress: the Trust was taking on responsibility for community and environmental issues outside its business purpose and scope of control. This made decisions overwhelmingly complex and they stalled. The Trust directors needed to see that their four key business objectives were a subset of the broader sustainability agenda of government.

Finding projects which fulfilled the four objectives, without adverse consequences, was a powerful turning point. It was the role of other government agencies to deal with issues that concerned the Trust, but which it had no authority or capacity to act on. When this was discussed and agreed with the directors, the sense of relief was palpable. The barrier to progress was gone.

During our work, we examined the range of projects they were required to fund, delving deep into their characteristics and how they related to the Trust's core business objectives. We were looking for the critical parameters of the projects that would matter most to decisions. We identified an elegantly small set of indicators to address multiple objectives across a range of project types. For example, one indicator was: "Volume of water available for storage and not held for (potable) consumptive uses". This indicated water available for environmental flows, flood storage capacity, and water for irrigation purposes.

A process was then developed using the small set of three assessment criteria: Did the project application fulfil the core business objectives, was it technically feasible and could it realistically be delivered? If the project fulfilled these three requirements, it was eligible for funding. Indeed, once the tool was developed, funding started to flow to eligible projects.

The key insight from this experience was that the metrics within the tool weren't the most important thing – it was the clarity the tool brought to the process that was most valuable. In fact, the tool was perceived as so simple but powerful, the Trust made it available online for project proponents to self-evaluate their projects, reducing the number of less worthy submissions, increasing transparency of funding requirements, and reducing the Trust's workload.

Rule 2 – Apply a tool early for the best results

Our experience tells us that tools with the most impact are those that influence design thinking from the *outset of projects*, rather than rating or comparing options once they're developed. These are tools that help identify "what the right project is". While it's possible to identify the most sustainable of several options by applying an assessment tool, this can also deliver the "least worst" alternative and not the "best solution available". That is, one of the options will achieve the best assessment and will be judged as the most sustainable, but may have serious deficiencies.

Rule 3 – Process is vital

Tools are not about a mechanical calculation. People apply sustainability tools and work with their outputs. A tool applied by a single person in isolation is a recipe for irrelevance. The more the process engages team members and draws upon their expertise, the greater the potential for influencing design decisions.

Sustainable design requires a little more effort from design teams as it demands innovative thinking during the design process. The role of a tool is to apply a wider lens to the design context, and to flag a broader suite of criteria to influence the approach. Cultivating innovation and creative ideas with practical merit is fostered through collaboration and working with different thinking styles and expertise. A good process will really get the most value from people and their technical smarts.

Effective facilitation of this process is an important ingredient – it's not a meeting you need but a workshop.

Rule 4 – Avoid hardwiring and complex software

Tools that are hardwired into software packages are less transparent and the decisions being made are not easily tracked. While the visual presentation of outputs may be slick and professional, the substance and detail are often hidden. One aim of the whole process of applying a tool is for all involved to see and understand the logic of the final outcome, and how the assessment contributed to this. Outputs that are objective and defensible are crucial. The criteria, assumptions, logic and process should be totally transparent to all.

Rule 5 – One size does not fit all

Generic tools and standard criteria that are applied as a standard recipe to different contexts and projects are ineffective at best, and at worst avoid scrutiny of the attributes specific to the project. Tools need tailoring to meaningfully reflect the particular context.

Take the example The approach you take to tailoring a tool is critical. This was well demonstrated by the experience of a national Defence department we worked with on a planning project. The key question was *"How will sustainability issues impact our business now and over the next 20 years?"* A real challenge was being clear about the scope of the problem, and defining criteria that were consistent with this, which could be expressed in language that was meaningful to Defence staff.

We needed to think holistically about the scope. The essence was identifying where changing social, economic, industry and environmental factors could constrain the business of defence – training, maintaining and deploying military capability. One issue this process uncovered included noise. Many bases were close to growing regional towns that were gradually encroaching into the noise buffer. New aircraft had different noise profiles that were likely to exceed the noise limits, making some bases unusable for training purposes in the future.

Really understanding the department's business, language and context made it possible to structure and apply the tool in a way that went to the heart of the problem in meaningful terms. Yes, the project had many complexities, but all projects have complexities – and the sustainability tool we applied brought clarity and focus to the most material factors.

Rule 6 – Communicating for impact

It's worth repeating the obvious. In the end, tools don't make the decision – people do. So *how* the tool's outputs are communicated becomes a key element in the process. How should information be presented for maximum impact; to be informative and engaging? What level of detail, metrics and comparisons will be most convincing, and really bring focus to the material issues? Complex and detailed material should be distilled into information that conveys the essential message in easily communicated formats. The graphics and visual outputs will be powerful in communicating both the story and key outcomes of the assessment in a simple but credible and memorable way. Be bold and add some creative graphics to your robust findings.

Finally, after thoughtful and smart use of a sustainability tool, the decision is made, the strategy or design endorsed, and implementation is underway. Time, resources, budgets and even reputations are being invested. So how are progress, achievements and other outcomes best captured and reported? We explore this in our next chapter.

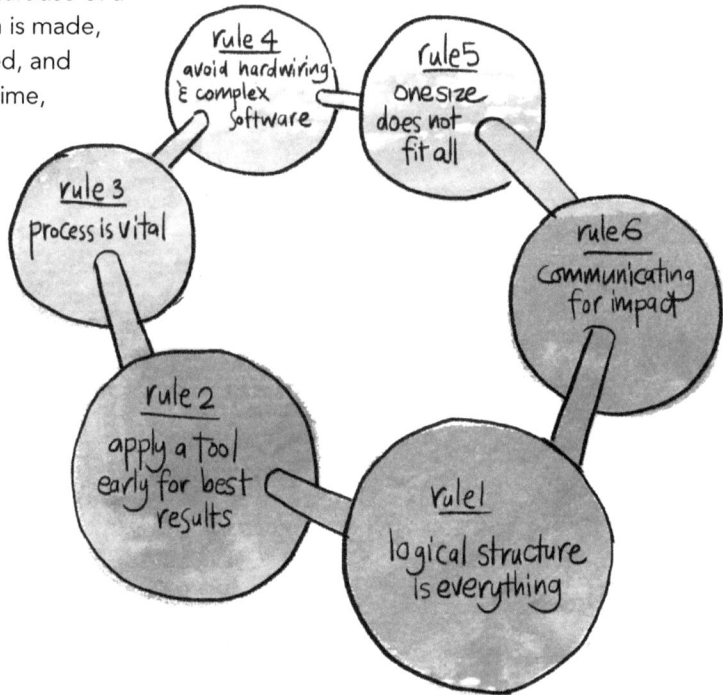

rule 4
avoid hardwiring & complex software

rule 5
one size does not fit all

rule 3
process is vital

rule 6
communicating for impact

rule 2
apply a tool early for best results

rule 1
logical structure is everything

USEFUL QUESTIONS

- **What do I want to achieve with a sustainability tool?**

- **How does the tool help to fully understand the problem and build a sound logic to the response?**

- **What process will make the tool's application most effective?**

- **How can I use the tool and its outputs to influence others?**

Thirteen

Reporting progress

An unread sustainability report has no value.

Reports should look forward, as well as back.

The most important audience may well be those in your organisation.

"Reports are too long, too backward looking, too complex, too general purpose."

Lois Guthrie, Technical Director,
International Integrated Reporting Council, 2012

"Twenty of the United Kingdom's biggest media companies… meet every quarter for discussion and debate. One topic discussed in 2010 was reporting on sustainability and corporate responsibility (CR) – who does it, how, and who reads it?

The results were fascinating. Almost all the companies at the table produced some kind of CR or sustainability report. Most spent 3 to 6 months on its production – collecting the information, writing, working with designers and auditors.

And yet no one had any real confidence that it was read by more than a few people. Nothing: no readership surveys, only a handful of hits on the website and little or no feedback… The real problem is that the average CR report is a composite, multi-purpose document, designed to fulfil several functions and consequently doing none of them well."

Simon Hodgson, Managing Director of Acona, blog on guardian.co.uk, 15 March 2010

Analysing and reporting evidence of sustainable business practices to evaluate the investment attractiveness of organisations will become the norm rather than the exception. While stock markets are reacting negatively to socially and environmentally harmful behaviour,[41] companies are attributing greater value to acquisition targets that have managed their brand and social licence effectively.[42] For example, one research study found that preservation of the social licence to operate can explain the difference in the valuation of two gold mines identical on traditional key valuation variables: the amount of gold in the ground, the cost of extraction and the global price of gold.[43]

Ensure reporting works hard for your business

For many organisations "triple bottom line" reporting represents their first foray into the world of sustainability, and the vast majority of the largest companies in the world now issue public sustainability reports. Indeed, for some businesses sustainability reporting remains almost the major sustainability initiative, often prepared by the PR department at arms' length from day-to-day core business. Reports are prepared to respond to the requirements of customers or rating agencies, or for "stakeholders" because it's the "thing to do these days". We find this both curious and regrettable.

Consistent with the trend for more reporting, CFOs are taking on a larger role in sustainability reporting. Clearly, CFO concerns centre on raising the quality of data and eliminating risks associated with distributing bad data. The move toward integrated reporting – combining sustainability data with financials – is also spurring this push for higher quality data.[44] Rather than just reflecting on past performance and current initiatives, many reports are looking ahead, explaining their supply chain risks and how they're preparing for them.

41 C. Flammer (2012) Corporate social responsibility and shareholder reaction: The environmental awareness of investors. *Academy of Management Journal*, July (online)

42 Quote from Andrew McLeod, General Manager of Communities, Communications and External Relations for Rio Tinto

43 W Henisz et al (2011) *Spinning gold: the financial returns to external stakeholder engagement*, working papers, Wharton School

44 http://www.triplepundit.com/2012/01/sustainability-reporting-headed-preview-ey-greenbiz-survey/

Sustainability monitoring and measurement systems should not exist in isolation. As we have argued throughout this book, sustainability issues are not peripheral but integral to business continuity. Goals and key performance indicators (KPIs) should be set as part of strategy formulation and business planning. Each sustainability initiative should be monitored and evaluated against these KPIs, not only for the delivery of outputs but also for outcomes – real business benefits. **If sustainability reporting is not providing the information required to drive real business improvement, then why bother?**

Most reports we read are missed opportunities and we see many organisations failing to realise the full value of their public sustainability reports. Typically, sustainability and similar reports are viewed as "stand-alone" projects by senior management and continue to be assembled each year as a "one-off" project, rather than being seen as a more strategic tool linked in to the business. What would be the benefit if indicators, performance and systematic sustainability reporting were embedded into an organisation's operations to create a "live" sustainability report that would provide feedback and influence decisions during the year? We know it would (or should) influence strategy and decisions in important ways and we wonder why more don't do it, given their investment in design, assembly and distribution.

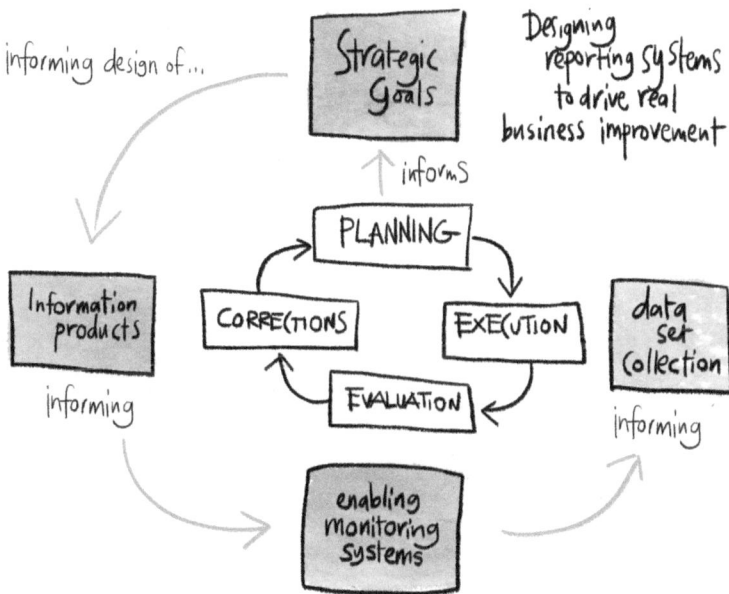

Reports have less impact when seen as a stand-alone product, and not linked to the organisational systems that drive real improvement. The connections are not difficult to establish.

Reporting publically

It's worth saying a few words on sustainability reporting for external audiences because they are the main vehicle to present an assessment of an organisation's performance against sustainability-based criteria. Sustainability reports are a tool for communication, evaluation and improvement, as well as for setting future priorities. We've developed and verified numerous sustainability reports across different industry sectors and recognise a common shortcoming in many. They often lack honest, rigorous and objective assessment of the most challenging issues confronting an organisation. There can be a timidness to admit shortcomings – but if we can't admit shortcomings, how can we work on them?

Who's your audience?

There is often little thought about the primary audience for a public sustainability report, which means it can be difficult to define what you want the report to achieve. Who will read it and who do you want it to influence? Audiences can include staff, media, government agencies as well as community groups, and some will be more important than others. Defining your target audience and what you want to achieve with your report provides its focus and shape.

If reporting should fundamentally support real business improvement, then surely it follows that a key audience for sustainability reporting must be the management team and Board of the organisation.

We believe the second audience for reporting should be shareholders and staff, communicating to demonstrate business achievements and benefits, where problems were encountered, that there is ongoing commitment and the steps that the business will take to make further progress. With a commitment to learning and ongoing improvement there should be no problem in acknowledging areas of poor performance; indeed, it's through mistakes that we have our most valuable learning moments. **Overly positive reports always create scepticism in the minds of readers**, and staff in particular are adept at seeing through it, so don't undermine trust and credibility. Be honest.

When companies are required to report by rating agencies, clients or investors, transparency and accuracy are equally if not more important. Indeed, given the declining trust in government and business and growing interest in risk management and responsible business practices by investors, the demand for public sustainability reporting is only likely to grow. The current trend is towards greater alignment of traditional financial reporting and reporting on ESG topics. With the trend for greater integration with traditional financial reporting, boards and management teams must be more vigilant in disclosure of material environmental matters as required under the International Financial Reporting Standards (IFRS) and related regulations.

Ultimately, sustainability matters are relevant to organisational strategy and performance in the short- and longer term and thus need to be monitored and acted upon. Materiality assessments will become more important, as will valuation of ESG information and its impacts. Reporters need to be clear about their audience and why reporting is being undertaken, particularly in the absence of consistent disclosure rules and reporting standards across jurisdictions. Reporting must be harnessed to support business improvement.

Take the example The inaugural sustainability report we prepared for a national chemical company had major operations in six states. Senior management wanted the report to highlight and acknowledge their performances and also direct a spotlight to under-par performance. The reporting structure we developed reported the performance of each state operation against key indicators, rather than simply collating all data. The intent of this was not technical but to provide an easy comparison of the different operations. It worked. Regional managers could for the first time compare their activities with others and clearly see where improvement was needed. Major improvements were noticed in the following year. One important audience for the report was the staff, and it was designed with this in mind.

We were also diligent to ensure the report provided an objective assessment of the company's achievements and identified areas for improvement. The organisation's lawyers somehow got involved in things and judiciously deleted all reference to any shortcomings. The sanitised version that was published saw it lose credibility in their industry – because everyone knows all organisations have areas of poor performance.

This in itself is not the issue. Recognising the problem and charting a course of action to improve is what builds credibility and confidence in your organisation. In our experience, public reports that provide an objective assessment build trust and confidence. The "greenwash" accusation is unfortunately an accurate description of many. A lost opportunity in our view.

In South Africa, integrated reporting is now mandatory, and pending European Union regulations are expected to make similar types of non-financial reporting mandatory in the near future.

CFOs are picking up on these changes; Deloitte has found that 60 per cent of CFOs at large global enterprises (with average annual revenue of US$17 billion) believe that sustainability challenges will change financial reporting and auditing.[45]

What data is important?

There is rarely a shortage of monitoring and data on all sorts of issues – but often not on the really important indicators central to an organisation's priorities. When we start on a reporting project we often hear this from senior managers: *"There's no shortage of data for you to work with – we're a data-rich organisation!"* But when it comes to assembling the relevant information on key performance indicators, we often find that meaningful data to work with is scarce. A project manager of a regional urban authority developing sustainability indicators for the fastest growing region in the nation captured this problem when he said to us, *"Use the data we've got rather than the data you need."*

Data often reflects what was important a decade ago and what is required by regulations. Air quality, water and noise monitoring data are cases in point. They exist in spades. In contrast, few metrics usually exist on the community apart from the funding of various activities or the numbers of meetings held, or the progress of community reference groups. Most information is descriptive, which are interesting but rarely shed light on important questions such as *What are the community outcomes we are aiming for?* The question and issues posed by a thoughtful sustainability report in the 21st century demand new information to really understand past performance.

But it is not all about what happened over the previous year. The better public reports are a combination of past performance, and future priorities and direction. They need to look forward as well as back.

45 Deloitte Research (2012) *Disclosure of long-term business value. What matters?*, Deloitte Services LP, New York

USEFUL QUESTIONS

- **What data about performance would you really like to have?**

- **Who is the audience for your public sustainability report? Why would they read it – and would it meet their expectations?**

- **How would you set up a report to drive change and improvement?**

Fourteen

- - - - - - - - - - - - - - - - - -

What now?

A final recap

We've spoken a lot about change in this book: changes in the way we define risk, value and success as well as the changes to approach and action required for an effective response, and finally, the changes that people and organisations are actually making to address the challenges they face.

These challenges are now evident globally and you will increasingly recognise them in your neighbourhood, workplace and city.

What once were intangible issues and externalities are being quantified and translated into prescriptive requirements through legislation, regulation, financier guidelines and supply-chain specifications.

Pursuing "business as usual" and delivering more of the same will fail by a long margin. Political and business leaders as well as investors, regulators and communities are increasingly agreeing the time for action is now.

Sure, this presents risks and challenges, but this is just one side of the coin. The other is opportunity and reward.

Ignite new thought and action

Smart leaders, formal and informal, at all levels of organisations are energised by these challenges and opportunities. They know that rewards await the people and organisations that provide solutions to society's problems. They are integrating social and environmental considerations with financial objectives to reshape their businesses and projects, ensuring they are fit for purpose, fit for the future.

So this book is not an environmentalist's "call to arms". It is a call to *thought*. To be mindful and challenge each other in the way we approach, design and ultimately implement projects that affect communities, cities, regions and even nations for decades to come.

Our experience demonstrates that it is never a waste of time to pause, however briefly, to reflect on our objectives, intent and approach. The path to achievement of better outcomes is not hard, expensive, or lengthy, but surprisingly straight forward.

The essence of opportunity is the way we think

Collaboration and systems thinking unleashes a more expansive and holistic perspective, which paints our projects and organisations in a more realistic light as part of a wider system with important connections and relationships at various scales across the landscape.

"Joining the dots" is central to avoiding short-term, narrow and siloed projects and solutions that are designed in isolation from connections and relationships that determine their real value. Innovative, even transformative solutions flow from this approach of questioning assumptions, actively seeking integration and intentionally "designing out" problems and creating enduring value. The adage "you get what you ask for" rings true.

Of course we recognise that thinking differently doesn't just happen, nor does implementing the best ideas. It needs a good process, some useful tools that stimulate strategic thinking and translation to action, a collaborative approach and effective facilitation.

We have aimed in this book to provide a practical focus and useful insights based on real experience and examples. We hope it has interested, motivated and even inspired you.

And this is where the book ends. With you.

What you do matters

You have a choice to be an active participant in deliberately constructing a preferred future, or a passive onlooker in a future that others shape. What is your design intent? What is your positive legacy?

We leave you with a simple message.

Everyone has the capability for smarter thinking, better design, and more fulfilling work.

The proven ideas and insights and the transformative solutions they offer are within reach of us all.

We can do so much better.

www.ingramcontent.com/pod-product-compliance
Lightning Source LLC
Chambersburg PA
CBHW041453210326
41599CB00005B/236